More Praise for
YOU HAVE A NEW MEMORY

"Such an addictive and mesmerizing book. The true heart of this brave and deeply observed book is in its tenderness. Within its pages you will find love in the apocalypse and hope in the doomscroll."
—Frankie Barnet, author of *Mood Swings*

"Reading Arata feels like staying up late with your most perceptive friend, the one who somehow always manages to articulate exactly what you've been feeling about the internet, about relationships, about existing and consuming in this pre-apocalyptic world. Her observations are so piercing yet playful, they will make you laugh, wince, and feel less alone. For anyone who's ever experienced the quiet thrill of a DM or the hypnotic pull of an endless feed (hello, all of us), this book is a must-read."
—Alexandra Chang, author of *Tomb Sweeping*

"Arata's shimmering debut not only showcases a unique breadth and depth of thought, but also serves as a road map for seeking out beauty in a world that always feels like it's ending."
—Priyanka Mattoo, author of *Bird Milk & Mosquito Bones*

"Arata's gaze is keen and gentle, graceful and curious, and there is no subject too large or too small for her—it's all here: the unbearable terror and beauty of life as it is right now, and as it has always been. To share the space of Arata's eyeline is to be changed."
—Alexandra Tanner, author of *Worry*

"Arata's skillful and endlessly entertaining guided tour through the Very Online Posts of our past made me laugh, shudder knowingly, and think more critically and rigorously about what it means to grow up on social media."
—Emma Specter, author of *More, Please*

**YOU HAVE A
NEW MEMORY**

YOU HAVE A NEW MEMORY

AIDEN ARATA

GRAND CENTRAL

New York Boston

Copyright © 2025 by Trash Cat, Inc.

Jacket design by Dana Li. Jacket image of face from *Joan of Arc*, 1879 (oil on canvas) by Metropolitan Museum of Art, New York, USA/ Bridgeman Images. Jacket images by Getty Images and Shutterstock. Jacket copyright © 2025 by Hachette Book Group, Inc.

Hachette Book Group supports the right to free expression and the value of copyright. The purpose of copyright is to encourage writers and artists to produce the creative works that enrich our culture.

The scanning, uploading, and distribution of this book without permission is a theft of the author's intellectual property. If you would like permission to use material from the book (other than for review purposes), please contact permissions@hbgusa.com. Thank you for your support of the author's rights.

Grand Central Publishing
Hachette Book Group
1290 Avenue of the Americas, New York, NY 10104
grandcentralpublishing.com
@grandcentralpub

First Edition: July 2025

Grand Central Publishing is a division of Hachette Book Group, Inc. The Grand Central Publishing name and logo is a registered trademark of Hachette Book Group, Inc.

The publisher is not responsible for websites (or their content) that are not owned by the publisher.

Grand Central Publishing books may be purchased in bulk for business, educational, or promotional use. For information, please contact your local bookseller or the Hachette Book Group Special Markets Department at special.markets@hbgusa.com.

Print book interior design by Jeff Stiefel

Library of Congress Cataloging-in-Publication Data

Names: Arata, Aiden, author.
Title: You have a new memory / Aiden Arata.
Description: First edition. | New York : Grand Central Publishing, 2025.
Identifiers: LCCN 2025001083 | ISBN 9781538767597 (hardcover) | ISBN 9781538767610 (ebook)
Subjects: LCSH: Arata, Aiden. | Internet personalities—United States—Biography. | LCGFT: Essays.
Classification: LCC PN1992.9236.A73 A3 2025 | DDC 791.092 [B]—dc23/eng/20250114
LC record available at https://lccn.loc.gov/2025001083

ISBNs: 9781538767597 (hardcover), 9781538767610 (ebook)

Printed in the United States of America

LSC-C

Printing 1, 2025

For MG

CONTENTS

Pink Skies Over the Empire (Introduction), **1**

America Online, **9**

On Vibing, **31**

My Year of Earning and Spending, **47**

What's Meant for You Won't Miss, **58**

The Museum of Who I Want to Be for You, **72**

How to Do the Right Thing, **96**

In Real Life, **145**

An Endless Soundless Loop, **182**

It Ends and It Ends and It Ends (On Glory), **205**

Author's Note, **223**

Acknowledgments, **225**

YOU HAVE A NEW MEMORY

PINK SKIES OVER THE EMPIRE

(INTRODUCTION)

SCATTERED ACROSS A craggy limestone steppe at the union of the Dyje and Svratka rivers, the twenty-six-thousand-year-old Paleolithic site Dolní Věstonice yields the earliest ceramic technology in human history. Among its ruins: the remains of two walled kilns and over ten thousand fired fragments that were once cats, bears, wolves, women. Fourteen thousand years before the production of utilitarian ceramics such as drinking vessels and fifteen thousand years before the dawn of agriculture, humans made themselves. The figurines were crafted from whetted loess before firing; their cracked remnants are a matte gray-black, dusted with siliceous ash, dinted by pointed tools and fingernails to demark eyes and ears and the creases of flesh folding over hip bone. The Venus of Dolní Věstonice, a four-inch faceless figure, is embedded with the cosmic swirl of a child's fingerprint.

The thing about the statues of Dolní Věstonice is, they were never meant to last. The material itself is remarkably resilient—lab samples survived six hours in boiling water and eighteen hours of soaking with no loss to stability or durability—and yet of the ten thousand unearthed pieces, only one figurine of a wolverine and a few gray pellets were discovered intact. The rest followed an unusual breakage pattern of "rough, stepped, and branching fractures," according to the 1989 *Science* article that first examined the ceramics' anomalies. After subjecting replicas to trampling, weathering, and "mechanical breakage," archaeologists found that the only way to reproduce the unique fissures was to induce thermal shock via a precise and impractical firing practice. As *Science* put it: "Such properties of the Dolní Věstonice loess as the near-zero drying and firing shrinkage, low thermal expansion, and relatively high porosity make thermal shock an improbable event during firing...Thermal shock did not occur accidentally but required intentional effort and practice." The archaeologists' work concluded that the ceramics had been created and destroyed as part of a social or religious ritual, what a contemporaneous *Washington Post* article called "prehistoric performance art, or perhaps even a religious ceremony." The sizzle and shatter, the noise and shrapnel—perhaps, the archaeologists posited, the fragments were used to divine the future. A sign of human life: an icon you can keep in your pocket, an impulse to obliterate it. An impulse to search the wreckage—then and now—for meaning.

When my friend texted **Keep me updated on your eta we're launching a car off a cliff at sunset**, I was already edging my way out of the asphalt sprawl of the city. Since the beginning of the incorporated city of Los Angeles's relatively short history it's been billed as a string of destinations, which induces a sort of radical subjectivity in which—geographically, socially, emotionally—wherever you are isn't where you need to be. You have to be able to tolerate a certain placelessness to live here, a kind of psychic distortion; always just beyond containment, hydrologists and geologists still debate whether or not Los Angeles is a desert. Everyone I know has a backpack of Band-Aids and space blankets in the front hall closet. Everyone I know is always halfway out the door. I keep sneakers by the bed. I am asked to discern, at any given moment, what I would abandon and what I would save.

I recently saw a commercial for a home security system that had rebranded as a special moment–capturing system. No longer limited to the catalyzation of Nextdoor uproar and the apprehension of package thieves, the commercial demonstrated how users might record cute dogs and dancing delivery drivers and Grandma's face in fishbowl as she rings the doorbell. So much in life is lost. The only way to hold on to anything, the commercial suggested, is relentless surveillance. It would be facile to act like the pre-internet era was a mindful utopia in which everyone lived in the present tense, but I wondered, as on-screen a bride was showered with flower petals and then the image slowly zoomed out to reveal I'd been watching her on an anonymous voyeur's phone, whether somewhere along the way there's been some small seismic shift, all the furniture moved an inch to the left. Rather than creating or seeking experiences worth recording, there's a compulsion to preserve everything—a lack of trust in human discernment, maybe—and a vague objective to return at some unspecified later point to pick through the remnants, to archaeologically excavate some self that matters.

Maybe surveillance anxiety is why my camera roll, at the time of this writing, contains 90,785 files. If I took exactly one second to look at each image in my camera roll, it would take more than twenty-five hours of continuous viewing; I would be my own twenty-four-hour surveillance system. Texts—both incriminating and inconsequential—and memes, quotes, receipts, sunsets, pets, nudes, insurance cards, blurry finger ghosts. Six identical shots of a tiramisu doomed to remain unposted because when the high of documentation wore off it felt grubby and sad to post about tiramisu: to act so smug over so little, like I wanted someone to feel *jealous* of my tiramisu, because why else post on the internet except perhaps also loneliness and maybe I was aching for someone to wish they were with me, and how craven to post a core wound under the treacly guise of abundance, and anyway the tiramisu melted as I photographed it and by the time I got the flash right it looked like sea foam on dog shit. Leading a life with intention is supposed to be this noble act, but a life lived online *is* intentional. It's just a different intentionality: all that potential energy, and then a tremor or a spiral instead of forward propulsion.

Anyway, the drive to the ghost town is a geographical straight line and an ontological loop. Whenever I pass roadkill, I say a prayer for it—which, if you're praying, it's already too late. *Please may that possum not have suffered.* Sometimes while driving I feel overtaken by the vibration of the highway and a velvet grief descends on me without warning, a curtain dropping mid-show. It wasn't supposed to go like this—humanity—but I don't know another way. I will never see most of the photos in my camera roll again.

My friend is a musician who met her partner, a ghost town renovator, while exploring caves in which to record an album. (Caves and mines are geographically similar, if spiritually divergent, and the ghost town has both.) The ghost town sits between the mostly accurately named towns of Lone Pine and Death Valley, and just above Owens Lake. For a brief period in the late nineteenth century, the ghost town and Los Angeles were roughly the same size. Then, in 1913, William Mulholland—renowned city founder, namesake of one of LA's most famous thoroughfares—rerouted Owens Lake into the Los Angeles Aqueduct, diverting its snowmelt to the city. Los Angeles swelled, and the ghost town atrophied. Owens Lake is a salt flat now, a great basin of dirt and salt and shallow pools of mineral sludge; for nearly a century it was the largest source of dust pollution in the country. The dust hit me around Lancaster. It rose spectrally from either side of the highway and diffused the daylight so that the landscape was a flat gradation of pink and tan and the mountains grew dimmer as they neared the horizon, like the world was subtracting itself layer by layer in front of me. Roadside outlet mall signs, stacked one atop the other, were stained brown as a pack-a-day smile.

After two centuries of abandonment, the internet raised the ghost town from the dead. Nearly two million YouTubers follow my friend's partner as he explores the warren of mines, drags a couch and Christmas lights into one of the tunnels, and restores the rotting general store. He is warm and personable, as normal as any internet celebrity who lives in a haunted mine could be. When I arrived, the ghost town was an assemblage of the half-dilapidated memories of wooden buildings, snow-dusted chaparral, trucks and Jeeps, ATVs, propane tanks, and a sheet metal chapel with a Christmas-light star. It is a cosmic stutter: discovery, displacement, violence, extraction, fallowness, and now, discovery again. There's Wi-Fi on the mountain. Stepping out of my car, I pictured the confrontations between pickaxed phantoms and radio waves, the quavering exchange of energy.

A long-haired kid in a Carhartt beanie pulled up on an ATV and beckoned me to follow him. Up the mountain, in the middle of the dirt road, squatted a flat-tired gray sedan. This was our sacrifice. I hadn't asked why a car, or why a mountain, or why sunset. I had some idea about roadkill and oil derricks, but the real reason was that it was what they had on hand. A trio of YouTubers who adapt beater cars for four-wheel drive had recently visited the ghost town, and when one of their projects turned junk on them, they'd abandoned it. A famous car, then—a celebrity object, a jewel of engagement. A small crowd in winter coats took turns aiming rifles at it. Anyway, being a star just means your decay casts light on something else.

We made introductions. An acquaintance hugged me with one arm, a pistol in his other hand, and kindly offered to show me how to load his gun. I smiled for photos, then tried to look serious as I extended my arm.

Bullets ripped through the clean high-altitude silence, warping the air long after I pulled the trigger. The driver's side door groaned and drooped from its hinges. A photo op. Clay shaped like a woman, just to burst into pieces.

At the cliff's edge was a small square of AstroTurf, a freezer bag of golf balls, and a putter. Beyond, the sun hovered over miles of rocky mesquite wilderness.

The Carhartt kid sat in the driver's seat with the door hanging open. Someone else pulled a Bobcat up behind it and slowly pushed the car forward. The sedan's windows were blown out, the bumper hanging at an angle. Jittering along together, the car and the Bobcat looked like segments of one big metal bug. The Bobcat's lights created a yolky circle around the car, and we followed the light to the cliff's edge, laughing.

The car shuddered and stalled. The kid got out of the driver's seat, retreated to viewing distance. The Bobcat reversed over a boulder and tipped into the air, lights spinning. It came down hard at an angle. It centered itself, then charged forward. The car teetered only a moment. It flipped, graceful as a diver, into the cold, clean air.

To feel at one with the world is to feel free. To feel free is to feel powerful. To feel power is to have entered a dynamic—to have put oneself at odds with the world again. And so it goes. One hand on the fiddle and one on the matchbox.

When the car hit the rocks, the thud of impact was swallowed by the canyon. Laughter ricocheted, quieted. The boys hopped onto ATVs and drove donuts until they flipped over. The dust hung around their circle of noise, trapping the light like a halo.

I walked to the edge and looked over. What a pointless thing. The car had done a nosedive, landed nearly vertical, and stayed that way, dug into the earth in an ancient outcropping of stone. It glinted in starry flashes from the light of a phone: a mirror, an idol, a highway cross.

AMERICA ONLINE

I WANTED TO touch the Starbucks barista's cheek. It was sometimes smooth and sometimes stubbled with blond bristles that reminded me of how ancient civilizations told time with sticks in the sand. It was always 7:00 a.m. where we were, between the Robeks and the triangle park studded with dewy purebred dog turds. The triangle park's official name was the Village Green; it was a traffic median trying to be a town square. The barista had a mom haircut that was trying to be a Kurt Cobain haircut. *I've been listening to Nirvana since I was a baby*, I wanted to tell him, and he'd say, *Wow. That's why you're so mature.*

History constructs itself frenetically like a million moving colored dots create static on a screen. Who can pinpoint the origin of anything? In Starbucks while my mother idled at the curb, I rolled the hem of my uniform skirt and eased the elastane of my thong up over the starched khaki lip. You could say, then, that when the Starbucks barista inevitably fell in love with me, it would have started with the thong, which started with a sacred mother-daughter bickering ritual in a Limited Too dressing room, the carpet a swirl of green and orange flowers and vaguely crunchy underfoot.

You could trace the exposed thong—whale tail—to 9/11: directly, in that New York Fashion Week 2001 was interrupted by the towers burning, landing the fashion industry at both the geographical and cultural center of a new sort of crisis; and philosophically, in that the act of 9/11 begat the culture of 9/11, a series of paranoiac fantasies and ritualistic self-surveillance that, among other things, sought to correct what 9/11 enthusiasts saw as a decade or more of dangerous behavior. In response to intersectionality and homosexuality and the clang of patriarchy dismantling, the first few years of the millennium were the golden age of the Mean Girl. The Mean Girl took the safety pin from her earlobe and used it to bind the inner corners of her bra cups for better cleavage, raised a bottle of Mike's Hard to a hypersexualized yet philosophically conservative celebration of superficiality and vapid bitchiness: Abercrombie and freedom fries and white-trash-chic trucker hats.

On September 11, 2001, I was an elementary schooler in California watching my father watch the news on the little TV in my brother's room. It was the day of the class overnight to Catalina; I brought my sleeping bag to school, and at some point, the school decided to send everyone home, and somehow my name was passed over on the parent call list. Children were picked up, administrators departed, and I wandered the quiet school hallways, touching the metal locks on each locker one by one. Later, when witnesses had trouble expressing the devastation, they would speak of women's shoes: office heels littering lower Manhattan, from women who had thrown them off to run, or had been propelled out of them. Recovered from the wreckage, along with the shoes: 437 watches and 144 wedding rings. People will tell you these things don't matter—the watch, the thong, the wedding ring—like what lingers is less important than what leaves. In California, I unfurled my sleeping bag on the blacktop and waited for someone to come for me.

You could trace the Starbucks barista's love for me—once he fell in love with me—backward from the purchase of the thong, to the Mean Girl, to 9/11, to the dot-com boom and the nascence of reality television. Computer geeks became overnight billionaires and at the same time, with the right cocktail of magnetism and attention-seeking behavior, anyone could become a television star. An exposed thong: a celebration of class upheaval.

Desirability is a group project—a collusion and a collision of circumstance, luck, and not an insignificant amount of tragedy. At Starbucks, the center of my thong—the whale's body—was straight and taut: a divider of something. Before and after, maybe.

If you'd asked me then, I would have said the epicenter of whale tail is the asshole.

Someone from homeroom logged us onto an AOL chatroom. We were 19/f/cali. We were 21/f/florida. We were brunette. We were petite. We were home alone. We found someone willing—24/m/slc—and via messenger, we administered a hand job. We were in his blue car. He was pulling our long hair. He wanted us so bad. 21/f/florida spread her legs for 24/m/slc and I jiggled my leg so it occasionally touched the razor-nicked knee of the girl next to me. I pictured an entomologist spreading a butterflies' wings, pinning them into place.

When the little box on the screen flashed I just came, we typed, Me too. I came so hard too.

In the computer lab you could get school credit for dragging a paintbrush across a digital canvas or saving penguins from drowning by typing at an adequate speed or clandestinely cybering with strangers. You could, as I did, exchange erotic Pippin and Merry hobbit fan fiction emails with Melissa Pate. dear merry, as you are aware, in the bathroom of mordor, we had passionate hobbit sex. i had just thought it was a fling...you know...all about the sex. apparently it wasn't. love??? pippin.

If I was the raw materials of desirability shaped by hormones and history into some kind of art—outsider art, maybe—Melissa Pate was a slab of marble, cool and opaque. She had a freckled moony face and a short blunt haircut like the haircuts of my father's friends. She collected soda can tabs and carried around a pimply plastic gallon jug of water instead of a Nalgene with band stickers like the rest of us. Her strangeness was magnetic. The most beautiful girls in our class treated her with gentle awe, like she was a ladybug that had just landed on their shoulders.

If you were to trace the history of the erotic hobbit fanfic emails, you'd probably start with Friday afternoons, when we watched *Lord of the Rings* in Melissa Pate's clammy downstairs rec room. At some point, Melissa and I telepathically—like twins who die at the same time or lovers engaged in a folie à deux—decided that *Lord of the Rings* was a love story. By fast-forwarding through all the battle scenes, we could patch together a romcom in which a will-they-or-won't-they couple of hobbits escape various foibles and hang out in an anthropomorphic tree. We did this every week, pausing to debate lore, skipping through the DVD menu to select the director's commentary. Does it matter who emailed who first? There is no more sacred bond than a shared delusion. dear pippin, i thought we had a beautiful night together and can't wait to do it again. maybe we can film the fourth movie ;) love—no question!!!—merry

I wasn't on forums, didn't speak in the blossoming nomenclature of fandom; when I loved something, I loved it privately, shamefully, where no one could take it from me. My emails with Melissa were an exception. Pippin and Merry discovered each other's bodies. Frodo seduced Merry, threatening to hurt Pippin if Merry didn't submit to his sexy games, and then Frodo, that agent of chaos, emailed all the lurid details to Pippin. In the fallout, it was revealed that Merry and Pippin had been secretly married the whole time. Everything came back to sex. Not the specifics—the mechanics of it were half-formed, perpetually stuck at 30 percent loaded on the screen of my brain—but sex was the black hole at the center of every conversation. *Slut!* my friends and I said, punching each other in the arm for no reason, for fun. Or the reason was that women were always putting one arm around you and saying, *Honey, your thong is showing.* When I'd dressed as a Hooters girl for

Halloween, with a branded T-shirt and a tray of empty plastic cups and a lumpen sock-stuffed bra, the school librarian said, with real sorrow in her voice, "You look like a hussy." Which was the point. *Hussy* was pejorative, I knew—I briefly cried in the drama department bathroom—but the librarian leveled the insult the way animals attack when they're afraid. To address desire head-on, to control it: this was power. You could do the bad thing, or you could become it.

Most Saturdays I donned a bought-on-sale strappy red Betsey Johnson dress or a pair of stretchy black pants and a *nice blouse* and low-heeled sandals that were shiny except where they were scuffed along the inner toe from how I tripped over myself because I walked like a miserable zombie. My mom cut a check and ushered me into her station wagon or the station wagon of whoever was driving carpool that week. Bar mitzvah season was a circadian thing, like a season of love or a depressive episode. I sat in temple and watched my classmate or former classmate or summer camp friend become initiated into the secret clan of adulthood in a way I would never be, since I'd been raised half-assedly Catholic.

    I met Brian at Rachel Goldberg's, which by the standards of West Los Angeles bat mitzvahs was fine. It wasn't Jacob Weiss's inflatable golf course on the hotel lawn, or the *Grease*-themed party where Sammy Shepherd arrived by straddling the resplendent shoulders of two parallel motorcycle-riding drag queens. It wasn't the one with endless jars of candy where Morgan Waters gave Nathan Volm a hand job under a table. Rachel Goldberg's bat mitzvah theme was *desert nights,* and so it entailed a Culver City dance hall decorated like a sensuous Birthright advertisement: filmy drapery; cut-out camel silhouettes; the warm, yeasty scents of pita and puberty.

I was doing what I privately referred to as *loser laps,* circling the party because my friends were with people I hated or who hated me. Sitting by yourself where anyone could see you—where someone's mother might ask if you wouldn't like to dance with someone's little brother—was suicidally shameful. I could spend hours pretending to be on my way somewhere. I passed Brian by the catering trays and by the bathrooms and it dawned on me that he was doing loser laps, too, and then he said, "Hi."

I looked at this other loser—his thin face and floppy hair—and felt something akin to metal elevator doors sliding shut. The heavy, smooth snap, and then sinking. Earlier in the evening, Rachel Goldberg's bat mitzvah tarot reader had turned up my sweaty palm and told me I'd be lucky in love.

Brian was the son of a family friend visiting from Portland. He, too, was made uncomfortable by the team of adults dressed in black who'd been hired to dance with us as if they were our friends. His voice got higher when he was happy. I tried to feel lucky in love. That elevator feeling: going down.

Brian asked for my AOL screen name. I was a system of pulleys and levers. I was a gash of pink thong on hip bone.

There was an internet before me. There was a humming beige cube and then an orange cube through which I could see the veins, like a wrist held up to light. There were verdant velvet hillsides and black oceans with glimmering parrotfish. There were rolling waves of solitaire cards that broke over my tiny face forever. But nothing was *for* me. My life was controlled by a pantheon of powerful but flawed gods, like in Greek mythology: parents, teachers, VH1 countdowns, *CosmoGirl*. As in mythology, the divine and mundane were constantly in conversation. The powers that be were obsessed with homeland security and teen blow job parties and achieving a very long, flat torso. Everything was a panic. I watched videos about chatroom predation and getting Elizabeth Smarted. I watched videos of horny stepmoms whose trucks were stuck in the mud. I watched the first few seconds of a beheading video before realizing what it was. I took a quiz to reveal my dating style (*shy n sweet*) and flipped the page to an article that invited me to pour soda all over my meal after a few bites, so I'd stop eating. My mother signed me up for a junior body bootcamp with two other unhappy classmates and an instructor who believed shin splints to be an issue of willpower, and in celebration, it seemed, *CosmoGirl* suggested I pair my long torso with a newsboy cap and flirt with my local lifeguard.

The internet for girls—AIM, LiveJournal, chatrooms devoted to horses and diet tips and cybersex—was a world our flawed gods couldn't penetrate. Before it was ruined by hateful murderer-virgins, the online manifesto belonged to teenage girls.

Though the LiveJournal website was a flat corporate blue, there was room for minor customization. My profile picture was a Microsoft Paint approximation of a narwhal, my background a tiled infinity of a low-resolution Velvet Underground photograph. My manifesto was homework and sleepovers. A good manifesto is a little clingy, prone to ornamentation; a little like a thong. I'd read *The Perks of Being a Wallflower* and a middle-grade British series about girls growing into their tits and riding around on Vespas, and as a result, my LiveJournal was insufferable. honestly, the world is such an amazing place for no reason at all sometimes, and i think that if you slow down and look closely at things, it's easy to see that everything about this place is just incredible. so go outside and enjoy your freedom, enjoy the sun and grass and sidewalks and all the life in the world right now, enjoy everything. Occasionally I would throw in a French word to sound worldly.

The writing was bulky, ineffectually gesturing at some childish idea of sophistication, but its radicality lay between the lines: It was a right to artifice. There was nothing remarkable about me—nothing special enough to justify my existence—but if I posted enough for my twenty-eight friends, the meaning of my life might come together, the mundane made lapidary. Better than the right to exist: the right to be someone else.

I smoked pot out of an apple in the park. I went to a punk show at the all-ages venue where you could order a bowl of white rice and watch some guy from Tulsa spin a microphone in circles by its cord. I went to an indie show in Echo Park and watched girls in feathered headbands get the band's screen names. I smoked clove cigarettes outside an IHOP and wondered when my life would start. I wrote in my LiveJournal, i'm so young and free.

I was mostly a good student. I believed, generally, that there was a point to everything, to geometry and racquet sports. I tempered the voice in my head that told me I was going to die. I had an English teacher with repulsive pillowy lips, and so as self-harm I envisioned myself kissing him. I attended an academically rigorous all-girls preparatory school: a school for the empowered daughters of powerful people, change makers, future women of ambition. Never mind that ambition was uniquely irrelevant to our demographic, the children of rich people. Ambition meant wanting the right things more than anyone else.

I wanted the wrong things. I wanted to unclasp Pippin's cloak with my stubby hobbit fingers. I wanted to be kidnapped and held for ransom to punish my parents for favoring my little sister. I wanted to introduce the Starbucks barista to Death Cab, and I wanted him to cup my face in his caramel-syrup-scented hands. When a friend's mother asked what I wanted to be when I grew up, I'd answered honestly that I wanted to be a weather girl: to look beautiful and talk about wind and planets, to be the least necessary member of the news team and be loved for it. I was heartbroken to learn of the rigors of meteorology.

Melissa and I watched *Lord of the Rings* the day I got my braces off. My retainer was too big for my mouth, or my mouth was too big for my retainer. I couldn't stop thinking about the microscopic gaps between the twisted wire, where food might stay forever. Over the soft lull of a far-off battle, Melissa showed me where to hold my tongue. "Say it again," said Melissa, and so I did:

"Thamwithe Gamgee is a thlut."

* * *

We swabbed the insides of our cheeks and piped lysis solution and ethanol into tiny tubes. I ended up with a viscous clump of white goo that was apparently my DNA. The other girls and I transferred the goo into dainty glass vials on thin ropes and wore them as necklaces. There were islands of trash in the Pacific. There was a husband on television who murdered his wife, and then called his mistress from her memorial service and pretended the background noise was fireworks in Paris.

The best time of day was 4:30 p.m., when no one asked anything of me. I lugged my enormous backpack uphill from the school bus and microwaved a Marie Callender's personal chicken pot pie and watched the drama where Las Vegas detectives huddled over murdered strippers until my brother came home and changed the channel to the sitcom where the man hated his sex-crazed wife. My favorite was the reality show about the construction worker pretending to be a millionaire. Twenty women pretended to love the construction worker pretending to be a millionaire, because they thought he was a millionaire. The construction worker felt terrible about it, manipulating women like so much dirt. He said this to the audience via voiceover as a woman licked whipped cream off his spoon in slow motion, maintaining eye contact.

When someone logged onto AIM, it was accompanied by the creak of a door opening. For large stretches of time the door never creaked and no one was online except the SmarterChild bot. You could ask SmarterChild if it was horny or tell it to kill itself, but that felt wrong to me somehow, like burying a Vestal Virgin.

They were destined for ruin, sure, but that didn't mean I had to dig the hole. Instead, I liked to craft a veneer of unavailability in the form of an away message—*~*~*it's a hard day for dreaming again*~*~*—and wait for a door to open.

Most days, Brian messaged me before I could post my away message. Wuts up? :0) When he messaged me, it felt like those mornings when I rolled out of bed and fought with my sister over who gets to pee first and brushed my teeth and pulled on my uniform polo, and then woke up—I'd only dreamed I'd been awake. I had to do it all over again, in the immediate sense and also in the sense of *This is the rest of my life. Just this, again.*

"He's so annoying," I told Melissa. It was some terrible late summer, the Santa Anas blowing sparks. The sky was muted and gray in the daytime, and ash clung to my eyelashes. We'd stripped off our uniform skirts to reveal novelty boxer shorts—cartoon hearts and chili peppers—and sat side-by-side on her bed, writing each other erotic emails. Melissa turned away from her laptop and toward mine. In the chat box, Melissa typed, This is Aiden's boyfriend Merry.

Earlier that summer I'd been to the beach, and in the sand, I found a photograph. It was tarnished and spotted with milky emulsion. The scene was outdoors, at night: a foreground of leather- and denim-jacketed men's backs. The closest figure stood with a can of Pepsi and a backward baseball cap stitched with what I didn't yet recognize as the Confederate flag. In front of the men was a wooden stage strung with colored lights, with a tarp stretched along a line of metal poles to create a backdrop. On this stage were women. The photographer captured the dip of an auburn-haired woman's bare breasts, the pale curve of her ass as she shimmied out of a pair of jeans. Next to her, a blonde in a pink sequined g-string faced the audience. I have a very early memory of *Playboy* splayed across a leather chair at a family friend's house: pages of gauzy bangs and mesmerizing breasts and bright smiles. The idea that you could be so beautiful that you would simply be tucked away, like Thumbelina, like the sort of secret that's a secret because it's valuable. There were eleven people in the photo I found in the sand, but the blond woman was the only one who wasn't obscured or turned away. She stood with her arms held straight out in front of her and her shoulders slightly hunched, like she was carrying something invisible but heavy. She looked at the audience, the camera, me. On her face was boredom or, more accurately, resignation.

I tried to picture how the blond woman felt about it all—the men, the photograph—but instead my mind conjured an image from *National Geographic*: a lone kayak in the middle of the ocean, a whale's submerged body beneath it. A massive looming darkness, imperceptible, but very close.

Pixels floated around the snowy nothing of the chat box. **Hello Merry XD.**

Once, in sixth grade, Allie Bergholt and I made an eHarmony profile for our lonely-presenting math teacher, who ate egg salad sandwiches at his desk and graded tests the day we turned them in. We compiled a dossier of eligible matches, presented it to him with smug munificence, and were called into an emergency meeting with the teacher and the head of the elementary school.

"Why did you do that?" Our teacher looked down at his hands as he spoke, his voice soft. I'd never humbled someone before. I read his softness as deference, but I was wrong—it was the specific anger of someone who has been embarrassed, adjacent to grief.

People—artists and religious nuts—will say creation is a choice, but it isn't always. Sometimes you can only see a choice in the rearview mirror. Melissa and I ate sour candy and downloaded a photo from her elementary school bully's Myspace and used it to make AOL and Hotmail accounts. merry. born in germany. moved to england when i was 1, moved to la when i was 7. enjoys: robots dinos silly boys n girls tacos long walks on the beach. friend me or don't.

I'd seen faith healers speaking in tongues on television, and they held their hands over the afflicted the way I held my hands over the keyboard that afternoon. I could sit very still and move my fingers slightly. I could tell a lie—an exhalation of breath, like any other—and watch my words ripple away from me. Who could say what that wave looked like when it broke on some distant shore?

Melissa messaged me from Merry's screen name, and I messaged her back, and then we messaged Brian to discuss what we'd been messaging each other. We watched *Lord of the Rings* less. We printed our conversations and bound them in a glossy white binder. I'd never been a girlfriend before. I loved the coordination of posting times, the way you could braid blue and red text into a conversation. Our previous erotic emails were pure fantasy; the version of myself that Melissa and I collaborated on was a new sort of real. When Melissa-as-Pippin emailed me-as-Merry, Pippin was capricious and occasionally cruel; sometimes she was Pippin and also a made-up side character named Jah-Jah who was constantly trying to break up Pippin and Merry's relationship, and I was inundated with emails calling me a cheater and a liar and a whore. Merry always won Pippin back in the end, but I sometimes worked myself into fits of quiet indignation over two imaginary entities having sex without me.

Melissa-as-non-hobbit-Merry wanted me to ride on his handlebars. He and myself-as-myself sat on the beach and harmonized the melody of a Grateful Dead song so well that we were interrupted by a record label representative. In Merry's LiveJournal, Melissa wrote, i'm the luckiest man in the world.

Melissa already had two LiveJournals, one real and one fictional. The latter—the sprawling epic of a shy but precocious photography student named Roxi—had gripped our entire class with its descriptions of darkroom infidelities and drunken reconciliations until a school administrator found it and forced Melissa to delete it. For our flawed gods, the shape-shifting terror of Satanic panic had sharpened to a digital point: the chatroom predator. One could speculate that this panic felt new not just because of the tech, but because to a vast swath of America, *stranger danger* was defined by distance: goths and gays and men of color, demographics America felt comfortable compartmentalizing. The average early internet user, in this American imagination, was educated, affluent, and probably white. When the screen's glow illuminated the predator, maybe the gods saw a little of themselves.

This was the extent to which we knew what we were doing was wrong—we were making ourselves vulnerable to online predation. I kept the white binder behind a wall of boots in my bedroom closet, next to a plastic handle of Popov and a garden gnome pilfered from the neighbor's lawn.

We weren't stupid. We followed the rules: no exact locations, no phone numbers, no meeting anyone offline. These restrictions also made it easier to lie. I found it upsetting that anyone would set their Sim on fire or drown them in the pool, but lying to Brian didn't bother me. Maybe I thought some part of him knew it wasn't real, in the same way I did and didn't believe it was real. If he did believe us, it wasn't because he was dumb or because we were deft storytellers; it was because the way we portrayed our real lives on the internet was just as strange and implausible. The fun party, the clever retorts during that fight with our parents: We lied all the time.

The world Melissa and I built was a pastiche of teen soap operas and young adult fiction, rife with improbable drama. I wrote Brian an anecdote in which Merry and I shoplifted from CVS and then made out in the parking lot. Merry told him about a party with balloons and dancing and cocaine, **Not that I do that shit**. Melissa and I dragged lines of baking soda across a paperback copy of *Jane Eyre* and took selfies next to it on a red Nikon Coolpix. Brian wished he could visit, and Merry said, **Someday**.

* * *

The construction worker's future wives smoked cigarettes in a Paris hotel room. They wondered, briefly, if his aversion to answering any questions of depth was a symptom of masculinity. They indulged in their shared romance, analyzing who he kissed, where, and for how long. "I'm so happy for you," they said, their smiles tense.

I wore my favorite dress—ruffles and spaghetti straps from one of Urban Outfitters' lower-end in-house brands—to a party, and then Nathan Volm spent the whole night lobbing soda can tabs at my chest. I kept talking to Melissa like nothing was happening, and tiny metal tabs kept hitting my face. I went home and took off the dress and scrunched it into a ball. I felt stretched thin and wound tight at the same time, like a Slinky, and like a Slinky I was supposed to remain flexible. I pictured a tapeworm curled inside me. I'd heard somewhere that if you had them, the only cure was to fast for a week and then sit in front of a bowl of warm milk. The worm, hungry as you were, would slither out your mouth. The horror of it—but also, the relief. The visual evidence. I dug a sewing needle into my cheek in search of impurities, gagged myself with a takeout chopstick to study my tonsils for stones.

Melissa blamed the bushes. She gestured tepidly at the hillside, like the Hollywood Hills were profuse with blackberry brambles. We sat on the curb, daylight fading behind us.

I picked at the hem of my knee sock. It'd gone gray from too many washes. "You were running with your arms in front of your face?"

Melissa lit a cigarette. I was thinking, *There are no Band-Aids the right shape* and *Even if there were, she wouldn't want me to.* Something like resentment burned in my gut—something uglier than care. A man had visited our school to talk about depression. "I was so worried they'd think I was a freak," he'd said. He didn't get it. The problem with depression wasn't that it was strange, but that it was mediocre.

Melissa said, "I think Merry's gay."

We coordinated the breakup meticulously. Merry was defensive, and then sorry. I was hurt, but ultimately, I understood. Melissa-as-Merry wrote over AIM, you know you're the first person i'd tell right? Waking life was filled with gaps, but the internet was seamless—I stepped into the stream of it, and it was as if I'd always been there and always would be.

At the diamond pendant elimination ceremony, the construction worker pretending to be a millionaire whittled his contestants down to two. One was an adventure-loving mortgage broker who, it was revealed late in the season, had in college modeled for kink magazines. Photographs of ankles bound in rope, stamped *Simulated Image*, flashed across the screen. "It makes you wonder, what kind of girls did Evan really end up with?" asked the former homecoming queen, who had tearfully faced elimination at the emerald pendant ceremony.

The second final contestant was a horse-loving substitute teacher. She was a nonsmoker. In her hometown package, the mayor of her close-knit community sat before an American flag and told us she was a very caring person. She hoped to sell one of her hard-won gemstone necklaces and send the proceeds to a Yugoslavian aunt in need of medical care.

The butler asked us to choose: Which woman deserves the construction worker pretending to be a millionaire's heart?

Melissa and I walked my skittish Sheltie around my neighborhood and thoughtlessly as a flinch, I kissed her. Somewhere, a cursor blinked. The air felt astringently cold and clean. We kept walking.

Later on AIM, I told Brian about a movie night with Merry's new boyfriend, how we'd all forgiven each other. I love my friends. Smiley faces floated around the ether. Later on LiveJournal, Melissa wrote of the day we walked the dog: Highly uneventful. Not necessarily unpleasant, but uneventful. I read that and thought of the closeness of our faces and of the tug at my wrist—the dog on its retractable leash. No matter how gently it strayed, there was always something at its throat.

I knew it was wires and zeros and ones, but it felt like it came from somewhere bad in me—like it was from the wet dark of my own mouth—when Brian messaged Merry, who was actually Melissa and me, and said, This is weird butttt...idk I don't want to say it.

I'd brought hard candies dusted in a chemical so sour they were rumored to be illegal in England, and the whole point was that they hurt. You held one in your mouth while your cheeks stung and your lips puckered and your eyes watered, until the sour coating dissolved to reveal a syrupy center so concentrated in its sweetness that it was a sort of agony, too.

YOU HAVE A NEW MEMORY

We wrote **say it**, and then Brian wrote **Merry I think I like you like you :X**

The room was rank with blue raspberry, dark except for our pale blue screen. The laptop's internal fan emitted an anxious hiss. I spit a sickly wet nub into my hand and looked at Melissa, her flinty face as she sucked air around her candy and let it out very slowly.

"This is amazing," she said.

On a metal bench in the yellowed Village Green sat two men, skate decks resting on their laps. I locked eyes with one and there was a moment of incomprehension—like there'd been a glitch, like he slid into a wormhole between the compilation CDs and the madeleine cookies and was spit out one address over—before I recognized the Starbucks barista. But also, I'd been waiting for him. When he invited me to see Modest Mouse, I'd know all the lyrics. Or he could invite me to huff whippets on a cardboard box in the Starbucks stockroom. I'd go willingly into his car. He could disorient me, lie to me, lock me in a basement, batter my body, drive me up the coast where the whitewater eats everything and passersby confuse screaming for the shrieks of gulls. The barista looked at me like he knew what I was thinking.

"Hi," I said.

He paused, then said something to his friend, who glanced quickly at me and then at the matted grass. My barista nodded, one tense jut of summer wheat stubble—time passing—and they shed their skate decks and stood and he curled his fingers into a floppy claw of a wave and with the clatter of plastic on pavement they rolled away, easily, like some breeze had blown our lives in different directions. He'd looked at me not with desire, but discomfort. Like I was the thing to be afraid of.

The construction worker shifted his weight from one foot to the other in the ballroom, which a production assistant had decorated with white pillar candles and fairy lights and potted artificial topiary trees. It was a sort of waiting room.

"I'm sorry I lied to you," he'd said to the virginal substitute teacher, who left without hugging him. Then the camera followed her as she wandered the woods outside the rental castle, conflicted and pensive.

"I haven't chosen you," he'd said to the fun-loving slut, who maybe gave him a blow job in the surfside suite in Cannes. "I just had a really good time."

A creak. A door opening.

The substitute teacher had changed into a demure blue chiffon dress to tell the construction worker that she'd been turned off by his inheritance the whole time. She loved the real him. The construction worker beamed. He offered her a diamond promise ring. The butler offered them both champagne and a check for literally one million dollars. The lie dissipated: Now they really were millionaires. "True love is a great treasure," said the butler. And then *The End* in white cursive on the glowing screen, the slow zoom out, the orchestral swell. The honest couple held each other, swaying tenderly.

* * *

Whatever mom or cop or god you thought was coming didn't come. Melissa had a mouthy friend who told him, eventually, I think, or maybe our plotlines were too circuitous, too sloppy and bold when he paused to unravel them.

Liar, Brian typed, once, and blocked us.

Melissa and I stopped talking about it, and then we stopped talking entirely. It felt wrong, speaking ill of the dead. Whether the dead was Merry, Brian, or something else, I couldn't say. Low-rise jeans, maybe. It was the end of whale tail. Now the most popular girls in school modeled for the understated T-shirt company—lucky girls with absent parents, or better yet, degenerate ones. The owner was a *boundary pusher*, but the shirts were so ethically made they were practically a penance, and the tenth graders' beautiful blank faces stretched across billboards along Melrose Avenue.

If we'd paid attention, we might have surmised that *Lord of the Rings* is a story about an object that isn't inherently evil, per se, though it's impossible for anyone to have it and not be corrupted by it—but we weren't paying attention.

Sometimes a door opened in real life and something fluttered in me. The dumbness of an animal: button, reward. Some quiet vigilance, to make up for everything I missed.

ON VIBING

THE FIRST TIME I was hospitalized for depression, the undergrad college into whose care I was released decided that the best course of action was a yoga retreat. I remember shockingly little of the retreat itself. It was in the Berkshires, in late September, and the leaves were violently, self-indulgently beautiful in their performance of death. I remember envying them. I don't remember yoga, or where I slept, but I assume both happened at some point. I remember padding down a silent hallway with terra-cotta sconces shedding shell-pink light. I remember attending a sharing circle in which I told the group that I thought about dying sometimes, and there was an awful awkward silence and then someone else said they thought about dying too, and then several people reveled in suicidal ideation, and the sharing circle leader became agitated and there were no more sharing circles that weekend. I remember clinging to the side of the hot tub in the women's spa and thinking about how the jets were so strong and so precisely placed that women—other, less enlightened women who humbly inhabited their bodies—must regularly use them to masturbate.

Years later, the most accurate way I can describe that place is a *vibe palace*. The endless earth-toned hallways, the hospital hush, the obliterating orgasmic drone of jacuzzi jets: The yoga retreat center was, and probably still is, a shrine to ambience. Even accounting for the cottony haze of depression, I should remember something about the yoga, right? The food? The women I lived with—did I live with other women at all? The Berkshires sprawl across two states; I could not tell you which one hosted my yoga retreat.

Whereas most vacations center around memory making, the yoga retreat cultivated an existential slipperiness, a detachment to experience repackaged as something like illumination. It was striking in its resistance to memory. To retreat: to back away. The whole point was to turn inward, to recalibrate, to heal through negative space. To vibe.

Vibrational energy exists; it is a fact of the physical world, unbound by history. *Vibration* derives from the Latin *vibratio*—to shake or brandish—and before that, the Proto-Indo-European *weip*: to tremble ecstatically.

The concept of vibes-as-life-force breached our collective consciousness in the 1960s and '70s as a celebration of utopian collective consciousness, or a watered-down, Westernized version of qi, or somewhere in between. Brian Wilson composed the 1966 hit

"Good Vibrations" as a nod to his mother, who believed that dogs barked at bad vibe emanators. The radical leftist collective Movement for a New Society's 1974 *Dandelion* newsletter considers vibes in its practical tips for organizing:

> While a group is new, when there is a likelihood of strong feelings, or when there are a lot of people present, a person may be designated as a "vibes" watcher—i.e. someone to pay attention to the emotional content of the meeting—make sure people are not interrupting each other, suggest breaks where there is a logjam or when people's attention is lagging, etc.

Vibes are the unit of measurement by which one's interiority mingles with the world around it. They are one's core essence seeping into the environment, like a loud laugh or a chemical spill. They're the spiritual equivalent of cartoon stink lines.

The vibe is a ghostly thing; unlike the parallel philosophies of animal magnetism and vitalism, a vibe does not require a living host. It is, by definition, insensible—impervious to perception via sight, sound, taste, touch, or smell. And yet, we sense them. The live concert has a limerence the album lacks; the most rational materialist prefers a restaurant with ambience. We know that there are colors and sonic frequencies outside the range of human perception. It would be bullheaded to insist that something only exists if it fits in our hands or line of vision.

If anecdotal evidence doesn't suffice, consider that in 1924, physicist Louis de Broglie expanded Albert Einstein's theory of wave-particle duality to include electrons and thus material objects. His conclusion, replicated in hundreds of experiments since: Everything—not just light, everything—is both a particle and a wave. Right now, you are sloughing waves into the atmosphere. You are vibing.

Vibes are also a seam in the social textile. They are associations communicated to and felt by others; by definition, their assessment is a dynamic collective endeavor. (If a lunatic is a minority of one, a vibe of one is just an opinion.) It's possible to like something with bad vibes, and to dislike something with good vibes; the systems that determine pleasure and repulsion are complicated algorithms, and vibes are just one of the data points. Some things with good vibes: dark wood, cumulus clouds, horizons, the way horses breathe, the Maillard effect, the magnetic hum of planets, sunlight through trees, the small spoons in coffee shops, heavy silk, running water, pastel toilets, the sound of a match striking, shrimp cocktail, certain types of despondency, someone else's earlobe in your mouth.

Some things with bad vibes: babies in streetwear, warm plastic, the gelatinous morning light after a night of insomnia, parking meters, static cling, desiccated sidewalk worms, cats in heat, blow dryers, wearing outside clothes in bed, casinos, fake plants, raisins, improv, the way drinking fountain water tastes like blood, baggage claim.

Some things that purport to have good vibes, but the vibes are actually bad: gray flooring in renovated houses, overly bred designer dogs, balloon arches, football mascots, music festivals, sleek white technology and pseudo-futuristic minimalism generally, Costco, cotton candy grapes, certain yoga retreat centers.

The yoga retreat healed me long enough to drop out of college and move to New York, where once a month I took a train uptown to a pink marbled office building where a birdlike woman wrote me prescriptions for psychosis and sugar overconsumption and general malaise. No one could settle on a diagnosis, but according to Dr. Shaw, I was generally disappointing and kind of scary, and I could be thinner, too. I'd been clipped by mania—not enough to believe I was a god or even a good person, but enough, Dr. Shaw warned me, that if I ever felt euphoric, it was probably sickness. Basically: My vibes were off. My frequency was freaking people out.

Dr. Shaw prescribed antipsychotics and Adderall, ostensibly to cancel each other out. (To vibe: to walk the middle ground.) She handed me brown paper bags of off-market pharmaceutical samples and asked me not to tell my insurance provider. The little paper bags were quaint. They possessed school lunch vibes. Nostalgia might be its own subset of vibe—an energy that skates the contours of inner and outer worlds, but also of present and past. Wandering through Manhattan with my unlabeled medications, picking through them like an 1840s prospector sifting his pan of dirt—vibrating it, if you will, so the dirt falls wayside and only the gold remains—I let the soft slant of the subway and the jostle of strangers sway me. I tilted my head back to touch the window and let the train rattle my brain like my brain was loose change. Who knew that the whole time, I was emanating life force? That etymological derivation, *weip*—some scholars posit it's also an early root of the word *woman*.

Perhaps our recent vibes renaissance—*vibessance*, if you will—is the organic progression of the same New Age wellness revival that resuscitated astrology and angel numbers. This renewed fascination with collective consciousness is reframed and intensified by the internet; the college zines of the 1970s feel almost oracular in their visions of shared energy, ineffable connection, and literal social networks. Lying in bed, the soft padding sound of your thumb as it flicks the glass of your screen: content ripples away from you, returns to you amplified. This is the magic of algorithms. You can watch someone vibe and feel yourself vibing with them. Data loops outward, laps itself, loses itself. In your phone, you feel yourself dissolving like a pill in water. To give yourself over to the collective, to drown in the stream: a beguiling way to join the revolution.

One difference between the vibes of the 1960s and vibes now is that the former are first and foremost a noun—a messenger, a closed loop between the entity from which it emanates and the entity that senses it. Vibes *(noun)* are relational. To vibe *(verb)* is to break the loop. To vibe is a quandary: an act of agency as much as it is passivity. To vibe is to go with the flow without sacrificing cultural capital; to be cool, but not threateningly so. To neither take nor offer. It's witness without crisis—the promise of a benign form of participation in a time when it is less and less possible to avoid complicity in harm. It's appealing, this ambiguity, this freedom from conviction. You can vibe anywhere, for free. In an era of immediacy, impulsivity, and aggression, to vibe is to hang back, percolate, and let your spirit surf some universal wavelength. In a world in which everything is packaged—reduced to brutal materialism and sold back to you—there is grace in honoring the ineffable.

There are online forums devoted to vibes that are alternately wholesome and cursed and think pieces that forecast vibe shifts with prophetic or paranoic rigor. Less overtly, the landscape of the internet can be its own sort of vibe palace. Objects materialize on my phone against seamless white backdrops. Disembodied hands whip soft tofu into wet nothing, push curls of butter through an antique silver press, wrap a ribbon around a candlestick. For what? For vibes.

We refabricate this online experience in the real world with the fervent construction of vibe palaces: the Van Gogh experiences, the Museum of Ice Cream. We even have temples in which to worship at the altar of bad vibes: escape rooms. These spaces are intentionally impermanent and often spring up within other liminal zones such as airplane hangars, warehouses, and shopping malls. Like the meditation retreat center, they function as oases of ambience; their purpose is existence itself, a space in which one can be and document the state of being.

Unlike the retreat center, these palaces are selfie traps, catacombs of carefully orchestrated branded backdrops and trippy lighting—but this only contributes to their shared core vibiness. In a series of studies set in labs and simulated museums, subjects who took photos on a camera phone or in Snapchat remembered up to 20 percent less of the experience than those who didn't. The act of photographing inhibited memories of the thing being photographed. One explanation for this dissonance might be that the subjects treated the camera as a prosthetic memory, an external hard drive for lived experience. However, memory impairment occurred even when the subjects had no expectation that they would access the material—when photos quickly expired, as in Snapchat, or when subjects took and then deleted them. Interactive or immersive installations comprise an entire industry devoted to memory corrosion: spaces whose real purpose isn't to exist, but to forget one was ever there.

Vibing is adjacent to dissociation, but it's not an exact correlation. Vibing is a *performance* of dissociation; to vibe is to say, *I am so sensitive to the world I must detach myself from it.* It's a little sophomoric that way. It's self-absorption at its most platonic, like you could consume yourself. Self-centered, like you could find some center in there.

Under Dr. Shaw's care, time became a thick stew. I slept for fourteen hours or not at all. I was in bed, and then I was throwing up on a subway platform, four hours late for the class I'd left my house to attend. I kept meeting people who claimed to already know me. I couldn't distinguish reality from dream from memory. When I told her this, Dr. Shaw suggested we simplify things, so she prescribed an experimental alpha-1 blocker called prazosin that would stop my brain from dreaming. Pharmaceutical companies are the great semantic philosophers of our time: They're constantly striving to give new meaning to old things. Prazosin was originally marketed to reduce blood pressure. No one knew why it stopped patients from dreaming, but it was popular among war veterans, and Dr. Shaw said they were developing a children's version, too.

I was then—as I am now—afraid of thrashing my way through life. Afraid of big vibrations: of earthquakes and breakups and sonic booms that make birds die mid-flight and fall from the sky like a plague omen. I am afraid of posting a bad take on the internet. I am afraid of the kind of sound that would hurt an animal's ears, but not mine.

Dr. Shaw never revealed who, or what, we were working toward; my brain had no vision board or five-year plan. It was nearly a decade before I found what I think may have been Dr. Shaw's psychopharmacological ideal: the stay-at-home girlfriend influencer. She is slim and vegetal, living off her boyfriend's money and the life force of algorithmic feedback loops, vibrating with internet attention like I once vibrated with prescription stimulants. She is depressive in ways I could only dream of, except she's actually thriving, and she'd probably be offended by my comparison. I know, logically, that out of frame there is a choreography of lighting and editing and analytics, but I'm beguiled by the girlfriend's dedication to the fabrication of a world of placid nihilism.

My favorite stay-at-home girlfriend influencer pads around her house in a cream sweatsuit. Her house is a white void: white walls, white cabinets, white sheets, white marble countertops, white coffee cups. Her bio is a flurry of clouds and swans. Her rich boyfriend is a powerful nonentity, an out-of-frame presence that allows her to exist as she does, often referenced but never shown. She's edited her videos so the sounds of her morning routine—fluffing pillows, pouring coffee—are heightened ASMR. And it *is* soothing, how her life is so contained. She speaks in a warm, pilled-out drawl that feels like a pointed response to the chipper prattle of the average YouTuber. To vibe is a response to girlboss productivity and to the girlboss's bratty little sister, the manic pixie dream girl. Both the girlboss and the manic pixie dream girl are measured by what they offer the world, how they might impress or delight it. Both require a lot of fucking energy.

I know nothing about my stay-at-home girlfriend, except that she likes matcha lattes with nut milk. Or maybe she doesn't even like nut milk, but the brand sent her a case. She accepts what the world puts in front of her, like a grazing animal. In response, objects manifest themselves for her: in one video she drips Paula's Choice sunscreen onto her cheekbones; the next post is sponsored by Paula's Choice. A breeze moirés its way across the surface of a dark pond. Paula's Choice sunscreen appears in my Instagram stories. Paula's Choice sunscreen appears at my door.

A vibe is both a record and a prophecy: Vibes shape behavior, and that behavior shapes vibes. The internet has magnified and diffused television's cult-of-personality politics; our allegiances adhere less to fact or policy than how we generally *feel* about someone or something. Our choices—from what we're ordering for dinner to whom we're electing as president—are deceptively driven by vibes.

Cognitive offloading, or the use of physical action to alleviate one's mental load, isn't inherently tech-driven—a *Trends in Cognitive Sciences* review offers the example of turning one's head to look at a skewed image, rather than adjusting the image mentally—but the expansion of the internet into phones and tablets has provided us an extraordinary offloading tool. Recalling appointments and phone numbers no longer requires cognitive lift, but neither does any hard fact. The invention of photography was revolutionary not only for its mechanical innovation but also for how it claimed the burden of representation. Presenting the world as it was had, for centuries, been the task of painting. With the advent of the camera, painters—no longer tethered to expectations of representation—reinvented the medium with impressionism, expressionism, fauvism, and cubism. Pocket-sized search engines have similarly freed the mind from memorization: better to just google it.

There's some parallel timeline, maybe, in which the ability to compile an endless library of facts brings us closer to truth. There's a world in which we are kinder and more understanding, because the mental and emotional space once filled with data is now concerned with analysis—the connecting, challenging, untangling, and synthesizing of said data. But as it stands, the sheer breadth and density of stimuli obfuscates whatever information we hoped to access in the first place. Per the BBC—reported over a decade ago—"In the course of a day, the average person in a Western city is said to be exposed to as much data as someone in the 15th century would encounter in their entire life." The result is all wave, no particle.

Consider the illusory truth effect, a psychological phenomenon by which repetition of information—whether factual or not—increases belief. A study in *Current Opinion in Psychology* notes of the phenomenon: "Repetition even increases belief in claims that are implausible or that contradict prior knowledge. Repetition also has broader impacts beyond belief, such as increasing sharing intentions of news headlines and decreasing how unethical an act is perceived to be." We see this play out on Facebook and vetted news platforms, in advertising and elections. Vibes are like morals, in that they're a code we all agree upon in intangible ways. We buy into them. The problem arises when vibes and morals are conflated. To make a choice from a place of vibes rather than ethics is easy; it's also devastatingly lacking in evaluation. It's radical avoidance, passivity masquerading as action.

My stay-at-home girlfriend's face has been plumped and smoothed to a state of anonymous beauty. Her hair is the color of milkfat. We get ready with her for events we never see her go to. She might not leave the house at all, except for the one time she takes us to the nail salon. "Nail day," she coos into the mirror, like she's talking to herself.

The salon is in an indoor mall. Footage of her sandaled feet traversing a beige grid of travertine tile is cacophonous with the sounds of passersby and whatever awful music is playing in Aritzia that day. In the salon, gloved hands shred my stay-at-home girlfriend's nails with a metal drill, wipe them with astringents, sweep them with bloody red lacquer. It's one of her lowest viewed videos, and I understand why; it breaks the spell, forcing us out of her world and back into ours. At the same time, the close-up camera angles, the disorienting cuts, the ferocity of the drill battering her acrylics into dust: She is her same distant, quiet self throughout. Her excursion captures a certain relatable withdrawal from reality—not a physical retreat, but a mental one. *You too can have a life like mine*, she seems to be telling us. *It's an internal frequency.*

I have been to many vibe palaces since the first, including but not limited to: a Dan Flavin exhibit; a James Turrell exhibit; a concert in a cemetery; an empty movie theater; a crosswalk glowing under the street pavers' tungsten lights; a rest stop in Arizona; a sensory deprivation tank, in which I couldn't stop thinking about my ears siphoning salt water into my brain; a doctor's waiting room; a gas station during a purple stormy dusk; countless humid crystal-laden storefronts of healers, psychics, and interpreters of dreams. I have worked in a yoga studio and said things like *How was astral projecting to perform reiki on that horse? Did he work through what he needed to?* (I never went to yoga.)

In these vibe palaces, I often found myself wondering: Can you shed bad vibes this way, like shaking dirt from a blanket? Maybe to vibe is to beat yourself with the stick of spirituality. Your muscles shake in exercise, in ecstasy, in terror, at any logical or illogical extreme. *I'm literally shaking.*

In de Broglie's 1924 experiment, he noticed that the behavior of photons depends on how the experiment is set up: They *do* act as waves, but only under certain conditions. The first vibe wave crested in the chalky aftertaste of the hyperconsumerist 1950s and the enduring horror of the Vietnam War, which reached its fifteenth year of bloodshed in 1969. Not just an era of fear, but weariness—the frayed edges of over a decade of hypervigilance. To vibe is also, perhaps, a generational survival mechanism.

You can flick from your stay-at-home-girlfriend to a dozen articles laying out how politicians and billionaires are taking an ice pick to the last remaining glaciers. If you're concerned about hurting people, or animals, or the natural world at large, every purchase and every social interaction is a potential harmful choice. Making things feels nearly as perilous as consuming them; writing this, I feel crushed by the possibility that I'm burning fossil fuels to chuck garbage into the Great Pacific Content Patch. Our edges softened, our thoughts diffused—a weak impression, a mark you can neither heal nor learn from, like that scar you got when you were a baby. Queasy panic for the individual, chaos for the collective. I am, at my worst, a personified microplastic.

Day in my life rebuilding after a breakup. My stay-at-home girlfriend's devastation, like her happiness, is muted. She listlessly wanders her white apartment in her white pajamas, beaten back by the waves of content creation, adrift without the lighthouse of some guy named Colton. She pours a green substance from a plastic bottle into a glass tumbler and drinks it with a glass straw. She lights a frond of incense and stands directly in front of it, perfectly still, her face arranged in a mask of wounded bravery. She heats unseasoned ground turkey in a Teflon pan.

A vibe is a weighted blanket on a dirt floor, a drone in both senses—an endless sound, a floating weapon. A fist with an empty center. taking life at my own pace 🫶, says my stay-at-home girlfriend, who is now a woman like any other. I trace her puffy face with my finger. For her to actually feel my energy, I would have to do something humiliating and insane, like leave cruel or horny comments on her videos. Is that why people act unhinged on the internet—to froth themselves into a frequency you can feel? I stop myself from recommending my yoga retreat center to her.

I got off my meds, and onto other meds, and off those too. I returned to dreaming. I went to a psychiatrist who wasn't Dr. Shaw, and she called me *the poster child for what's wrong with American psychiatry today*, and I took it as a compliment. My Saturn docked into its astrological center, home again; the vibrations of violent despair softened; my aura lightened at the edges like a spring dawn. I have been to therapy. I have vomited vast quantities of hallucinogens into a white bucket while an antivax raver whispered ancient wisdom in my ear, and I let her hold me, and I wept. To wail: Sound waves, the vibration of the vocal cords, the tingling of tiny hairs inside the ear. It's all the same. I drove to the beach, alone, and put my feet in the ocean.

If vibing, as we understand it now, is a dissociative response to nihilism, then the opposite of nihilism isn't optimism. The opposite of nihilism is belief. The first vibe wave spoke of heightened collective consciousness, harmonized frequencies, cruising the wavelength of enlightenment and inviting society along for the ride. A vibe: a space to step into with someone. A room of light. The point is resonance.

I have tried—am trying—to alchemize my vibing into noticing. To vibe *(verb, transitive)*. The function of perception is not just to consume information in the moment, but to use that information to build future moments; by failing to metabolize the present, we risk recursion, our lives an endless scroll. It takes a devastating amount of vulnerability to absorb information, to turn it over in your mind and allow it to change you. Vibe contamination, vibe synergy—is that what's happening when someone sees you naked and still wants to fuck you, or when you admit to your friends that you think you're a human microplastic, and they still want to go roller skating with you? When the stay-at-home girlfriend unlocks the screen door and lifts her face to the wind? I would like to be that breeze. I want to be the one that does the shaking.

MY YEAR OF EARNING AND SPENDING

June

I bought pink satin sheets from the internet for my birthday. When I told my boss it was my birthday, she apologized. I still looked great, she assured me over the phone, and then she gifted me a fifty-dollar voucher for a wellness center that called itself an *urban sweat lodge* and had already gone out of business. No one was co-sweating anymore.

My boss was a television showrunner who developed unviable network cop dramas. The studio paid my salary, which wasn't actually a salary—I used a complicated algorithm to fill out my time sheets with the exact amount of overtime needed to earn the amount of money promised to me when I took the job. This was impossible, and so to avoid being accused of fleecing the studio, I accepted less. The studio also paid for an office on the lot. My boss visited the office every few months, and I came in once a week to water the potted weeping fig. We rarely saw each other. She called sporadically with throaty proclamations, like a holy vision: a burning bush, marveling at its commitment to diversity when concocting another strict-but-fair inner-city police chief with a rough past and a chip on *her* shoulder. I felt doom most days, waiting for my boss to email me to tell me to patch her into a meeting, which was not technically possible on my model of iPhone. I sourced espresso carts for her five-year-old's birthday party and wrote "internal documents" that she reformatted and pitched as her own original episode outlines. She was a self-described *cool girl*. She ate bread and believed that harassment complaints were for self-victimizers unable to step into their own power. She had a pathological need to tell me how much she loved fucking her husband, a stay-at-home novelist-slash-photographer. One of my jobs was to make endless lists of presents for him. "A vibrating bra," she suggested, and so I was paid twelve-fifty an hour, plus a strategic unit of overtime, to research vibrating bras.

My new sheets felt like cling wrap but looked beautiful. I lay on them and scrolled through images of pastel seashell table lamps and glass bricks, chrome and mirrors and air. On social media this was called *cocaine décor*. To me the phrase *cocaine décor* evoked images of an iPhone laid flat on a toilet tank, or a fentanyl test strip languishing in a Sprite cap. At night the polyester sheets trapped the heat, so I had violent dreams and woke up scared and thirsty.

On social media, I started seeing advertisements for wavy mirrors and private rehabs and pouf-sleeved minidresses. I signed up for clinical research studies but never qualified. I bought a dress from an Instagram ad, pink silk with peach ruffles around the bust. I hadn't thought about my body in a while. I felt like pudding—sweetness ready to conform to any vessel—but the dress was erotically unforgiving: slightly transparent, pulling at the seams. I put it in the closet for later. Everything was for later.

July

I bought knockoff pink platform Crocs from AliExpress, and then name-brand pink platform Crocs from the official Crocs site after the knockoffs disintegrated under my feet in a jolt of summer rain. I bought a hot pink flower-shaped gemstone to shove into one of the Croc holes. I bought a blown glass pipe shaped like a lily of the valley, the white flower bowl twisting away from a translucent green stem, from a feminist glassblower's web shop.

I bought weed from a sinewy blond painter living in his mother-in-law's backhouse. He proudly educated me on which strain I'd be smoking, pointing out a neatly cultivated row next to some varietal of pepper while his mother-in-law sat under a beach umbrella in the driveway and ate tacos from a paper boat. Buying weed from a painter made me feel smarmy and anti-capitalist, though he told me that his most reliable customers were tech bros and stock guys who sparked their corporate creativity with DMT.

I got my weed dealer's number on the Fourth of July, from a Tinder date. I'd gone to this Tinder date's house and sat on his slanted roof above his metalhead housemates and a litter of feral kittens, and when he presented me with what appeared to be a real antique battle sword crisscrossed with lines of ketamine, my first thought was *Where can I buy a sword?* The fireworks were so close and so constant that they set off car alarms. Pitched forward on the roof, you could watch an explosion's full lifespan, from the Bic's halo in a cupped hand to the ash.

August

I bought a pink Champion bucket hat with a plastic face shield that zipped on and off. I bought a tripod with a ring light. I bought a subscription to *Enchanted Living Magazine*, which was full of recipes for berry treacle and essays on Dionysian repose and photos of women wearing fawn ears and velvet robes. On my laptop I kept a tab open to the auction of a 1990s Strattera pharmaceutical rep pen (**VERY RARE!**), visiting it every few days until bidding closed. The pen had a pudgy rubber grip and a curved plastic clip that seemed engineered to slip into one's mouth and when it disappeared I prickled with loss, even though I'd never been prescribed Strattera.

September

I got laid off. "I have to let you go," my boss told me, her voice hushed and sober. She was the detective at the door, waiting for the woman in the bathrobe to swoon and shudder against her. She was strong, to be so steadfast in my grief. I asked if she could keep me in mind if she heard of any open positions anywhere, and she didn't even pretend she would.

I bought a teeth cleaning on the last day of my dental insurance. The dentist was very hot, in a reality television contestant way, and very pregnant. The x-ray technician had never taken x-rays before. She apologized as she pushed the plastic tabs deep into my mouth, hitting my gag reflex and scratching the secret scars where I bite the insides of my cheek. The hot dentist jabbed at various milky apparitions on the x-rays and told me I needed five fillings. I couldn't wait, she said. My teeth were falling out, like in a dream. I asked if I could pay now and come back in a week. She pressed two Advil into my palm, closed my hand around them, and said I wouldn't feel anything.

After the dentist, I needed to clear out my office on the lot; it was also the last day my studio badge would work. I couldn't stop touching my lips, marveling at how swollen and soft they were—how smooth my skin was when I didn't know it was me. On the golf cart path behind Lucille Ball's dressing room, a security guard asked if I needed help. I made moist sounds, my mouth circling like a fish's. The security guard was concerned, and then suspicious. I raised my hands to my mouth, trying to manually manipulate the words, and realized I was drooling blood. I showed the guard my badge again and he called another guard, and together they watched me cart out my belongings: a few binders of scripts, my branded studio lot notepad, some brittle succulents.

I bought a plastic mouthguard. I bought a set of scrunchies with tiny zippers so you could hide drugs in them, even though I never went anywhere you'd need to hide drugs. I never went anywhere. I bought four months of probiotics because I forgot to postpone the shipping dates on my subscription—120 reminders that my flora was fucked up. I had the tools to save myself but refused to wield them. Sometimes I would see the probiotics in the fridge door when I was looking for fast-food condiment packets, and I'd double or triple the dose and give myself cramps. I couldn't cancel the subscription, though—what if I became someone who took daily vitamins? There was still time to change.

October

I signed up for unemployment. I lay in my sheets and grasshoppered my legs until the edges curled off the mattress corners and folded around me. I bought knockoff Louis Vuitton and Gucci masks from a van outside the Bank of America, on a whim. I didn't want to invest in masks.

    I bought a clear acrylic heart-shaped kalimba. I bought a Garfield Beanie Baby from eBay that arrived wearing plastic sunglasses and a tiny polyester T-shirt that read *Perfection is hard to improve!* I bought a tag protector for Garfield's tag. I bought teal socks with non-slip pads on the bottom, like you get in the psych ward, because I thought it'd be funny, but when I tried them on they just reminded me of the psych ward. In my early twenties I'd shuffled back and forth down the fluorescent hallways of Beth Israel, bloated with antipsychotics and plastic-wrapped bagels. I'd written in my journal: *Everything looks the same. If you don't move around an object you start to feel as though you are the object, the thing being watched. So you move as much as possible, which is not a lot.* I bought takeout from my favorite conveyor belt sushi restaurant and pushed it around the kitchen table, making soft whirring sounds.

November

My house smelled weird. I couldn't prove it, but I knew. I bought candles in slim glass containers, with scents like "amber" and "smoke." I bought scrub brush attachments for my Ikea handheld drill and spent nights drilling bleach into my baseboards. I bought persimmon bodywash from Japan that was specially designed to eliminate 2-nonenal, the fatty aldehyde better known as "old people smell."

December

An Instagram follower paid me $100 for lewds, which meant I didn't have to get fully naked. He sent me the money on Cash App and I put on a ribbed cropped tank top and black cotton briefs and took mirror selfies, careful to cover my face. When I messaged him the photos, he told me he'd pay me another $50 if I cleaned my mirror. I accepted his offer.

January

I bought a pink plastic comb from my corner bodega that broke in my hair, and I continued to use the half with more teeth on it. I wasn't wasteful. I loved leftovers. If I bought the wrong shape of coffee filter, I still used up the pack. Sometimes I saw an object online, and then pictured that object in a landfill, and then I had to buy it. It was like rescuing an animal. A set of salt and pepper shakers shaped like cowboy boots: a bonded pair.

February

I got a part-time contract gig at an ad agency, ghostwriting affiliate memes for million-plus-follower Instagram accounts. A CBD company's ideal customer was *28–34, disposable income, anxious, insecure.* An energy drink described their target demographic as *male, socially conscious, sarcastic, discerning,* illustrated by a photo of Elon Musk. A national sandwich chain forbade us from mentioning African wildlife, because their CEO had endured a big-game hunting scandal.

I trawled stock photo websites for the most relatable shorthand for the human condition. "Romantic honeymoon couple in love at beach sunset." "Thoughtful and beautiful woman, remember something." "Sitting circus clown holding your product in his hand." The experience economy used to be so small: love, heartbreak, dying in battle. People needed—I assumed—to get everything else right in real time. When they petted the cat, they had to actually feel their fingers in the fur, the warm contentment of another body.

Now everything could be demonstrated by something else. "Hacker hoodie man on computer with binary code": I am successfully clicking the crosswalks in a captcha. "Old-time schoolhouse with red apple on teacher's desk": I am trying so hard to be good but I don't know why.

MY YEAR OF EARNING AND SPENDING

March

I longed to sit in someone's passenger seat and see all the shit they'd stuffed into the door pocket. The wanting burned through me, crisped my edges. I bought a seasonal affective disorder lamp but felt exactly the same.

April

I bought a footlong Lucite clothespin, described as a *desk accessory*. I bought effervescent natural wines with silt pooling in the bottles. I bought a cervical spine alignment device that looked like a combination dildo-catapult. When my neck still hurt, I agreed to post sponsored content in exchange for a mattress.

I got Jill's email from a podcasting frenemy, and a day later she Zoomed me from a pale blue room with seashell art. She told me that she liked my look, and if I got enough affiliate engagement, she'd send me a mattress for my guest bedroom, too. I nodded in the style of someone with a guest bedroom.

Without the affiliate deal, the mattress would run over a thousand dollars. The most money I'd ever made at one time wasn't much more than that; despite only attending for one semester, I'd received a payout from a class-action lawsuit against a university, because the campus gynecologist had been a predator.

I created a professional Facebook page with a default profile photo and no description. I gave Jill permission to do whatever she wanted to it. I felt like a Sim. I didn't enjoy playing *The Sims* anymore, or even *Animal Crossing*. Now I only enjoyed buying frilly pastel dresses off adult baby fetish Etsy.

May

I refreshed the pages on my tracking numbers, savoring the suspended state of pending delivery. Now that I had a Facebook page, I could scroll Marketplace. I saw distressed leather sofas, secretary desks, cats in cat trees who were unaware their trees were for sale. I saw impossibly verdant AstroTurf beneath an Ikea utility cart. A fifty-five-pound box arrived. Inside the box was a vacuum-sealed coil of foam; it would become my new mattress in twenty-four to forty-eight hours, which was how long it took for the foam to expand and the chemical smell to fade.

I dragged my old mattress into the living room. I cleaned my room, filling a tote with frayed electrical cords and then hiding the tote behind the living room sofa. I bought a pink lightbulb with same-day pickup and watched a sprawling Technicolor sunset from the parking lot of the Burbank Lowe's.

I couldn't believe the mattress was free. The impulse to influence was humiliating, but also intoxicating, or maybe intoxicating because it was humiliating. I would become an object. I aimed to emit a certain entitlement to objectification: I could easily, happily, sell and be sold. In certain circles, perhaps, this is knowing your worth.

June

For my birthday, I made the bed with my pink satin sheets. I slipped my pink silk dress over my shoulders and arranged the waist tie. Had it ever fit? I followed a YouTube tutorial, dragging liquid eyeliner into a butterfly wing at the corner of each eye. A light formaldehyde scent clung to my hair as I secured it with a drugless drug scrunchie. I screwed in my pink lightbulb and set up my tripod. I turned on my ring light.

I stretched over the mattress I paid for in attention like a Flemish rabbit draped over a fruit bowl. The self-timer blinked. I smized and breathed in chemicals. I thought about 2-nonenal: the smell of time spending itself. I read somewhere that ants emit a special pheromone when they die. It takes two days to kick in, and when it does, the surviving ants practice a sort of ant funeral, where they carry the corpse to a heap of other ant corpses and leave it there. When scientists applied this pheromone to living ants, the ants walked to the graveyard themselves and sat with the corpses. They believed they, too, were dead. I tilted my head and looked into my ring light and smiled.

WHAT'S MEANT FOR YOU WON'T MISS

IT WENT LIKE this: Someone I met once three years ago was hiking. They packed the expensive sunscreen designed to smell like the cheap sunscreen of my childhood, and it was so effective I could smell it through the screen. Their Nordic nylon backpack glowed in a diffused dawn and the dog they could afford chased pine cones and there was so much chlorophyll in the air that if they hadn't overwritten the forest with a soft-problematic 1960s folk ballad, I felt I could hear the trees sopping up sunlight. My barely-an-acquaintance smiled and smiled and I pictured a person walking through the forest alone, grinning, and something about how demented that is brought me peace, but not so much peace that I didn't float over to a real estate app to browse Heath ceramic backsplashes and ebonized oak cabinetry, after which I flitted to

YouTube and let a tech mogul's tradwife show me how to open up a floor plan, and then I watched a survival tutorial on how to escape a sinking vehicle after crashing it into a lake not unlike the one my non-acquaintance was hiking to. When the tutorial turned out to be an advertisement, I sifted through my emails and then my influencer group chat for a low-stakes scam.

The other seventy members of the influencer chat would rather be called *creators*—a gesture at agency and expertise—but I like *influencer*; to me it sounds violent, Terminator-esque. Influence is a shapeless, pervasive force, difficult to pin down and thus easy to fear. We don't know who will influence us, or when. Something might change you and you won't even know it.

To stay in the chat, I was required to contribute three brand contacts a week—*quality* contacts, the moderator emphasized. No likes for likes, no affiliates. Nothing *desperate*. These were mercenary corporate sugar babies, open to any sponsor, impervious to the vitriol of boomers and incels and the *just jealous* masses. They promoted polyester milkmaid skirts and vegan hair vitamins and, once, a members-only NFT subscription service that purported to empower women in STEM by allowing them to create sexy nonfungible digital alter egos with changeable outfits. They were models-slash-actresses-slash-musicians. Their feeds were balloon arches and flower walls and thickets of hashtags. One had recently acquired an EDM DJ husband, and their wedding portraits were sponsored by a mid-tier suit rental company.

In Greek epics, between the lotus eating and the cruel conviction that return is possible, is *Xenia*: a social code, a standard of hospitality often translated as "ritualized friendship." What is the influencer, if not the ritualized friend? They exist in the expanse between intimacy and celebrity—a weird, sweaty place to be—performing approachability and aspiration in equal measure. Power traders of the attention economy, they mediate the sharp sleaze of advertising into something soft and trustworthy. Gifting is a touchstone of *Xenia*, and the influencer chat was an endless stream of *gifting opportunities*: free brunches, screenings, hotels, hard seltzers, sandals, perfumes, baby wipes, body bootcamps, nonstick cookware, no-show shapewear. Mile by mile, you could get a free ride through life this way: the flight to Vegas from one contact, for example, and from others the executive suite, the slutty dress, the seafood tower. In the economy of the group chat, nothing was exclusive and everything was transferable. It was almost Marxist, this open exchange of product at the expense of the company shilling it.

The influencers possessed an admirable unshakable confidence in their entitlement to free stuff, an ability to ask for more in a way that felt generous in its asking. There was a spiritual lean to everything, no matter the product—the gift was inherently mystical by nature of being free and for you, reinforcing the law of the influencer universe: You are worthy. I integrated this messaging by shuffling through manifestation podcasts at the gym, the elliptical on its lowest setting, my eyes searching for a serene middle distance that wasn't someone else's tits. For the duration of a binaural loop I might break through, succumb to the belief that happiness is a discrete and neutral object, dissociated from history or circumstance or systemic oppression. Through a combination of verbal affirmations and light tapping, I could—I *would*—shatter through the thin pane of this life and into my destiny. I would take what was already mine. And then my unaesthetic orthopedic running shoe slipped and the machine sounded its cheerful calamity, and I was aching and normal again, and none of the resistance trainers even looked up.

Public relations girls emailed me to raise my awareness for oil-minimizing toners, multitasking eyeliners, and a perineal massage moisturizer from a company called Rosebud Femme, whose marketing team seemed blissfully unaware that *rosebud* is already a genital thing, and that thing is *prolapsed asshole*. A skincare company invited me to a Pride event honoring *the dermatology community*, with a performance by Adam Lambert. A face gym offered a complimentary workout, gleefully promising that "trainers will use their signature massage techniques like knuckling, pinching, and whipping strokes." A courier delivered a three-course lunch and serum set to my apartment to celebrate the launch of a botanical skincare company. The pink gift bag was filled with rose petals; absorbed in my complimentary avocado toast, I forgot about them until days later, when they curled in on themselves and filled my kitchen with a powdery rotting smell.

I rarely emailed back, and initiated contact even less—not because I thought it was wrong, but because I was daunted by the challenge of writing a chipper email. But then someone I knew was in Italy again, and someone I didn't know had fireworks at her wedding, and someone I hated had everything, and

I filled out address form after address form for sheet masks and jawline-sculpting gum and self-cleaning litter boxes. Sometimes I responded to offers and sometimes I was the aggressor, supplicant and complimentary. I'd love to test drive for content consideration! In the moment I hit Send, I truly believed that I was going to post whatever they sent me. I pictured myself as someone aspirational: a flat lay, a self-deprecating caption. And then the product or the event arrived and it was a lipstick the cool mauve of a corpse, or it was a dinner at which I sat next to a public relations girl and sampled terpene-infused cocktails until the public relations girl, loaded on terpenes and recently single, dissolved over mention of Valentine's Day and wept into my mushroom risotto.

Historian and archaeologist Ian Morris draws from Marx, Mauss, and Lévi-Strauss to distinguish gifts from commodities thus: While a commodity is "an alienable object exchanged between two transactors in a state of mutual independence," a gift is "an inalienable thing or person exchanged between two reciprocally dependent transactors." What defines a gift is the relationship between the transactors—their dependence on one another. When the time came to post, I inevitably betrayed the bargain. I typed thank you 💚 and faltered. I held a bottle of now-with-less-forever-chemicals nail polish to the light and was struck by how strange my hands looked, the bulging knuckles, the one persistent dark hair on my right ring finger. My fingers had large pores. My palms were too square. Any Instagram witch could assess my lifeline and find it lacking. The tips of my nails were already chipped—would I have to follow up with a post about how I liked chipped nails? Would it become my brand? I moved quickly and thoughtlessly through the online successes of others, performing my rote rituals of inadequacy with a satisfying sting, but when it came to affirming my own abundance I ignored follow-ups, blocked contacts, and swore off grifting until the next desirous fugue attack.

One could spin this as righteous. There's a righting of the scales in a tiny scam: quiet justice in a world of MLMs and health insurance premiums. When talking about influencers, there's an impulse to default to words like *shameless*. But what's so great about paying for things? What's so great about shame? It's fair to say that influencing is, overall, perceived as the purview of women; women have long created industries at the edges of economy and have long been derided for it. To use one's beauty or affability or capacity for intimacy for the acquisition of power, and then to be shamed for that power, is an experience that predates gift economies. (In the epic times of *Xenia*, women *were* gifts.) And anyway, the rhetoric of manifestation—the rhetoric of happiness—is all about the diffusion of shame. Sometimes, like when I was emailed about an oil heiress's vegan clothing line, I simply wrote back, **pervert**.

But public relations girls talk. The address forms no longer led to packages. When I requested products, the responses were laced with suspicion: **What outlet is this for?** or more pointedly, **Oops! This list is full.** I risked excommunication from the influencer chat. These were the stakes when I received an email from an upscale sportswear company that promised a free outfit and spa day at the brand's wellness house. A doorway: a way back to where I belonged, where everything was free.

The Sunset Strip is one of those Los Angeles neighborhoods where no one from Los Angeles actually goes. It's embarrassing, overpriced, preserved in the amber of the early 2000s, all giddy consumption and dead-eyed sex appeal. It's where the girls stay in the LA episode of *Sex and the City*, and where the boys cruise in the opening credits of *Entourage*. There's the Coffee Bean where Perez Hilton once regularly camped out to draw cum stains on paparazzi shots of struggling women, and the Hustler store, and a jarring number of sixty-year-old men with ponytails and fake British accents who won't date above twenty-five. The Sunset Strip was the natural choice for an eight-bedroom, nine-bathroom, $24 million party house, which was, in turn, the perfect place for a sponsored influencer wellness retreat.

The invitation instructed me to wear only branded clothing to the event, so my first stop was the brand's flagship store in a Mid-City outdoor mall. The mall was overstimulating, the store's second-floor gifting suite inexplicably but delightfully overrun by influencers' off-leash purse dogs. Stained and wrinkled clothes splayed across the dressing room floor. The public relations girls smiled grimly through it, sifting through cardboard boxes of leggings in plastic envelopes. I tried on a series of humbling $70 mesh yoga shorts and opted for turquoise leggings and a matching sports bra. My public relations girl stuffed my street clothes into a branded tie-dye tote, along with a hat, scrunchie, and socks.

WHAT'S MEANT FOR YOU WON'T MISS

I bought a Sprinkles cupcake on my way to the car and ate it sitting in traffic. According to the scholars of epics, another thing that separates gifts from commodities is that the gift is inalienable: On some level, it never leaves the giver. It follows them around, an extension of their identity. Every item I'd been given was marked with the brand's logo, so when I put the outfit on I became the brand incarnate. In a haze of sugar and smog, I idly ran my hand along the inside edges of my purse until I hit a soft mass: two sports bras liberated from the dressing room, snuck past the event staff even though they were already free. I wiped the crumbs from my fingers on them.

The party house was actually two buildings, all concrete and glass, a minimalist contracting budget posing as minimalist design. There was a long driveway with a valet stand and two podiums, marked Air and Earth, a public relations girl behind each. I gave my name at Earth and was told to check in at Air. I walked six steps to Air, said my name again, and was instructed to go to Sea.

Between the buildings was a courtyard with a small stage on which six-foot-tall letters spelled out the brand name. There was also a coffee cart, and a white Jeep parked drunkenly across some grass. Women climbed on the Jeep in their sportswear, writhing, posing for photographs. Beyond them I found the Sea podium, where a public relations girl pointed me to one of the buildings.

In places of great wealth or beauty, I always felt like a fraud. I have short legs and buccal fat, and walking past the Jeep I was struck with panic that I would be tested on my wellness. Anyone could walk up to me at any time and ask me to do the splits. This was something I admired about my influencer peers: their ability to show up and fit in, to audience-test parts of themselves until they landed on something profitable. One girl's main account was the most successful of several exercises in identity, and her lesser projects remained public out of pride or apathy: a page devoted to a cat that she later relinquished in a bad breakup; a podcast page that hadn't posted in three years; a cooking vertical with a smattering of shots of meal-prepped shrimp tacos, the plates angled on a dark and unclean sofa and encircled in portrait mode migraine auras. She didn't seem to consider these abortive endeavors failures; instead, she used them to comment emojis on her main account. An outsider might say she lacked depth or integrity, but she'd never asked for depth and integrity. I, however, had asked for wellness and attractiveness and influence, and came up lacking.

My spa day turned out to be a fifteen-minute chair massage. My massage therapist was soft-spoken, worried about applying too much pressure. I hadn't been touched by a stranger in twenty months. After the massage, I let the therapist press various products into my palms, promising I'd promote them, warm from her hands on me, grateful.

Scam accomplished, I wasn't sure what to do with myself. I'd been too embarrassed to ask the group chat if anyone was attending this event; I wasn't even sure I wanted to meet them. I meandered to the gifting suite, hoping to secure a free yoga mat or more socks before driving home. A woman with an undercut and an earpiece stopped me. I couldn't go in that way, she said. I was supposed to be at the pool party.

On the other side of the building, sixty hot people had somehow known to bring bathing suits. They lounged in the grassy yard, kicked their legs in the sleek, narrow pool. At the pool's edge, a woman floated on Nike Air roller skates. A man in a taupe Speedo twirled, arms raised, before swan diving into a perfect downward dog. A DJ played the sort of benignly clubby beats you hear in car commercials. There were strategically placed mirrors with lines of people waiting to angle their bodies in front of them, phones raised. There were communal selfie sticks and event photographers wearing all black and wielding DSLRs. You could be photographed at any time, so guests paused mid-walk to perform headstands. They cheated out while they talked, like actors on a stage. They listlessly played table tennis on a branded table, pausing when they raised their branded paddles, smiling hopefully over their shoulders. Maybe the bathing suits were in the gifting suite. I tried to get in from the pool entrance, and another public relations girl told me the suite was "on pause." I should stay for the sound bath.

At a tent labeled the Mindful Masters Lounge, I signed up for an intuitive reading. At the pool bar I received a gin cocktail featuring an alkalizing mushroom powder that tasted like mud, and a chickpea quinoa salad bowl catered by a prestige health food store known for its $24 smoothies. The store was originally established in the 1960s because the founder believed that if people were better nourished, they would no longer tolerate war.

I watched a team of public relations girls greet a recent *Bachelor* contestant and her on-again-off-again fan favorite boyfriend. They were beautiful in real life, beaming for photos by the branded photo backdrop. In life, as online, everyone seemed sunny, flat, puppy-fun. Did I? I had a valet ticket and a sports bra and a cocktail. I was an ambassador of wellness. I sat alone in a patio chair and watched the gifting suite gatekeeper deny entry to another group of guests. I ate my salad, which was full of bitter greens.

The influence economy had only existed for a decade; the first generation of online personalities was just now aging out of the hot-girl market. A low-voltage resource anxiety ran through the pool party: What comes next? To rely on the market is to rely on one's marketability. You saw it in their faces. Anti-aging procedures purport to aspire to a more youthful version of the recipient, but the filled and Botoxed faces of the pool party were a study in posthuman beauty. They were literally *anti-age*: divested from time. An anti-aged woman could be twenty or sixty years old and occupy the same class of uncanny glassine appeal.

I felt it in the group chat, too. Lamenting her frigid audience engagement, one member purchased a doodle puppy and launched a new account the same day, with its own family-friendly brand voice: **Follow me for daily pupdates.** A true gift economy, Morris argues, "is above all a debt-economy, where the actors strive to maximize outgoings. The system can be described as one of 'altering disequilibrium,' where the aim is never to have debts 'paid off,' but to preserve a situation of personal indebtedness." The puppy's account was small but growing.

WHAT'S MEANT FOR YOU WON'T MISS

* * *

A few photographers huddled around the gifting suite entrance, among them a familiar face—a friend, kind of. We'd never interacted in person; we'd spent at least a year as characters in the LA Creative Cinematic Universe, exchanging story replies and eye contact across the gravelly courtyards of natural wine bars, slouching toward human connection. I messaged him, **are you at an incredibly chaotic yoga influencer event rn?** and he responded, LOL.

I realized, with horror, that I was about to be witnessed. Here I was: lilting my voice and asking about the brand's new magnesium spray, rolling on my spandex and driving an hour for a fifteen-minute massage.

My friend found me on the patio, and I instinctively crossed my arms to cover the noisy teal yoga outfit, the lengths I went to for an afternoon of aspirational grifting.

"How are you?" he said.

"Humiliated," I said.

My friend had been working the VIP lounge; apparently I'd been with the bottom-shelf influencers the whole time. He told me they'd made him change his clothes so as not to stand out, and to crop out anyone who wasn't wearing the brand head-to-toe. This was a three-day event, apparently, orchestrated to get the brand a few months' worth of content. Yesterday a teen had gotten wasted on mushroom cocktails and yelled "I am awakened!" during group meditation. The photography team was instructed to delete that content.

My friend also told me that the gifting suite was closed because all nine bathrooms inside the party house were completely backed up with shit. The entire house smelled like shit, in fact. It was coming up through the shower drains. I asked if he was fucking with me, and he wasn't, and we stood in silence for a minute, looking up at the uncaring glass exterior of the second floor, the wavy reflection of the party.

My friend who wasn't really my friend shuffled off to document three women with matching braided pigtails and I walked around the pool alone. I watched a woman evade the fridge steward, absconding with two fistfuls of Lärabars. I returned to the Mindful Masters Lounge to find that the *Bachelor* alumna had taken my intuitive reading slot. I sprayed myself in the face with sunscreen just to feel something.

A woman with a headset—there were so many women—announced that the sound bath was about to begin. Guests drifted to the DJ booth, which had been set with crystal singing bowls, and lay flat on the floor in neat lines in their matching yoga sets. The woman with the headset was our healer. The vibe was cheugy Heaven's Gate.

The healer started by announcing her Instagram handle. She told everyone to breathe. I filled my lungs with air. I sighed as instructed. A thing about scamming: either you get away with it because you're clever, or you get away with it because no one cares. Because you don't matter. There's an aching, godless loneliness in that.

"Imagine you're a star amongst the cosmos," the sound bath

healer said. It's so easy to lose respect for that which gives itself freely. I stepped up to an available mirror and took a selfie.

What's the point of an odyssey? To go home. I walked out of the pool party and into the courtyard. I couldn't get to the valet: a black trailer of porta potties blocked my path, backing slowly into the narrow driveway. A security guard waved me out of the way, onto the stage, where I stood elevated in the shadow of the giant letters and watched public relations girls guide the toilet truck, fanning it with their hands.

It was getting cold. A few drunk guests heckled the public relations girls. They were anxious about the photo ops, the aura readings, the yoga mats. When would the bathrooms be open? And the gifting suite?

"Soon," the girls soothed them. "You'll get yours soon."

THE MUSEUM OF WHO I WANT TO BE FOR YOU

THE HOTEL WAS famous for its photogenic escalators. They were encased in a steel tunnel that from any vantage point but inside resembled a human-sized trash chute, but inside the walls and ceiling were glazed with mirrored black glass shot through with coils of gold. The tunnel's opening was positioned at the hotel's entrance so the doors slid shut behind you with a hydraulic hiss and you stepped from the Lower East Side into the abyss. You floated to the second floor in a black-gold haze, surrounded by infinite iterations of yourself. The night I arrived, the escalators were broken. For a moment before I ascended I stood in the still-dark portal and watched the steel and glass pinball my wet breath back to me.

The front desk was a series of iPads tethered to wooden

pedestals with industrial wire. The rest of the lobby was the sort of commercial space described by Google Maps and only Google Maps as a *lounge*: errant sofas and Edison lighting and a wall of cubbies filled with inexplicable artifacts. I saw an oversized magnifying glass; a twee brass statue of a sitting cat; a replica of an oil painting of the Virgin Mary, her head bowed in bashful reverence. It was like the set of a 1970s film about the future. Some tan guy could come out in a Lycra leisure suit and a vaguely salacious forehead prosthetic and tell me the view of Earth is beautiful tonight. My room was accessed via elevator, and the elevator bank was flanked by infinity mirrors, bottomless carnivorous blue dots pulling you in.

Per the media of the past, the millennium was supposed to be all clean lines and snowy expanses, grids and vectors. Even the most visionary directors couldn't predict same-day delivery. Rideshares, kits with baby-talk recipes and single stalks of scallion sealed in airtight plastic: a million conveniences, if you were on the right side of the gig economy, which I was, in the selfie-themed hotel that was also an abyss-themed hotel. I was here for a meme conference.

I think it's important to say here that I didn't plan on becoming a narcissist. The app came to me—to us all—in an age of sincerity. We didn't collectively will it into existence with the purchase of seasonal lattes or the accumulation of student debt—the narcissism app materialized while we nursed our neon irony hangovers with saddle shoes and wooden owls, shrugged on the musty cardigans of indie purity, masturbated to bruised girls on Tumblr. The mason jars, the man who sat in the park with a typewriter: these were gestures toward *something real*. Big mistake, to conflate sincerity with truth.

The narcissism app launched a decade before I was invited to speak at its meme conference. The photogenic escalators hadn't yet been constructed. I lived across the bridge and hardly ever posted on the internet. I sometimes went dancing with an art handler named Milo, a quietly funny and obnoxiously handsome friend of a friend who most days and some nights bounced between the snowy walls of various tony riverside galleries. We'd litter a table with sweaty PBRs, and Milo would tell us who he'd installed that day, and while he spoke I studied his hands. Despite barely making beer money and living in a divided loft with four other artists-slash-art-handlers and no air-conditioning, Milo transcended the jurisdictions of criminal, social, and moral court: Milo touched the art. He cradled million-dollar masterpieces in his arms and swaddled them in moving blankets. He ran a white-gloved finger along the taut line of wire affixed to a gilded frame, and then stepped out for a smoke.

In the age of sincerity, in the bar with good dancing, in Brooklyn, there were two equal, opposing expectations that made your ears pop: to be the most special, and to be the least pretentious about it. You were unwittingly beautiful. You were a friend of the band. You were the last tenant before the first gentrifier. Milo's ability to fondle the Western canon—the opportunity, however fleeting, to break the Western canon over his knee—was a point of collision. His hands were veined lasciviously and flecked with plaster, and I could watch them all night: his thumb and forefinger pinching his cigarette like a sock hop bad boy; his fingers deftly flipping a plastic baggie inside out to lick its powdery residue; his palms on the hips of some other soft-spoken beautiful boy on the dance floor, the light above them strobing in waves, like the light, too, was falling over itself just to touch them.

While Milo approached immanence, I worked as a popcorn waitress at a movie theater that offered dinner service in your seat. As with art handling, the goal was to leave as little of an imprint as possible—to remain offscreen. You had to crouch down and creep around the theater so you didn't block a customer's view. Our service schedule was timed in accordance with the film's run time, so I watched the same disjointed ten-minute chunks of the same movies over and over again. By the end of a film's run, I knew snippets of dialogue forward and backward by heart, but I never saw the enemies become lovers, or the fighting words that catalyzed the big brawl. I fired another round into the ether of the point-of-service screen, and the prodigal son was home again. The theater lights came up early once and a patron caught me eating a tater tot off her plate. My job felt adjacent to touching the art, in that I was participating in the creation of an experience of art. It also felt like I spent most nights crawling through my rows with jiggly bowls of queso, staring into a string of strangers' crotches, which with the right soundtrack might resemble a string of small black holes.

Last year's conference was digital. In my laptop, a hundred faces blinked in little boxes as the moderators scrambled to mute our microphones. I'd decided to attend out of morbid curiosity, plus the narcissism app promised a special surprise and a gift bag. The special surprise was a visit from the platform's creator, a famously dorky billionaire, subject of tabloid and prestige paper headlines alike for his alien affect and his complicity in the corrosion of democracy. We were all creators at the conference, but he had created the app; he was the creator of the creators, which felt disconcertingly like deification. It was unclear whether he was teleconferencing to us live, or if his message was prerecorded, or the whole thing was computer-generated. His face was smooth—egg-like—and his tone upbeat. He loved memes, he told us. I tried to picture him looking at a meme and thinking to himself, *So true*. Our creator beamed into the camera and said he was proud of us. The gift bag was a box of self-care items: sugar-free gummy bears and bath bombs and sheet masks. I obediently unboxed it on camera, feeling a little like I was working for the tobacco company and the tobacco company sent me an air purifier.

I feel wary of a unified theory of memes, a proselytization doomed to grow stale on its herald's breath. At the same time, there are a few things I'd say, if I were proselytizing. I would argue that a meme can be a poem—an intertextual object that tricks its audience into playing with language, disrupting the relationships we project onto signs and simulacrum, et cetera. Those midcentury future films couldn't predict that little snippets of poetry would be co-opted by SunnyD and the CIA. Memes may be high culture's backwash, but everyone wants a sip.

THE MUSEUM OF WHO I WANT TO BE FOR YOU

I might draw a line between, say, the overpixelated, yassified bastardization of Squidward from *SpongeBob SquarePants*, and the irreverent-surrealist Dada art movement that emerged in the thick of World War I. Dada was a response to a proliferation of hyperrationalist, pro-war and capitalist propaganda in the European art world; it rejected reigning structures of reason on the basis that *reason* was an arbitrary set of standards set by those in power, a projection of objectivity that led to complacency, corruption, and violence. One could argue that memes might be the same sort of subversive regurgitation of capitalist media, a playful response to ruthless marketing and surveillance. Or not. To overanalyze memes would be a betrayal of their true nature, which is unremarkable—not as in *boring*, but as in *beyond remark*. What is there to say that Handsome Squidward can't say better?

And anyway, by the time the meme conference rolled around, what was a meme? Everything was *content*—a label so vague it gestures at nihilism, a medium defined only by its ability to be consumed. My content concerned wellness, which was to say, mental illness. On my profile, a sweet-looking caterpillar reared its head: *I believe that life has meaning—however, I fear the meaning of my life in particular is very stupid.* A swan paddled around a rococo bathtub: *Predictability is mediocrity. I am a sensual scholar. I ate a whole jar of gummy vitamins. I am banned from the Apple Store.* Garfield wore sunglasses: *I hate all days!* Sometimes I printed my content onto dad caps and T-shirts, and a few times, I'd been paid by an allegedly feminist sex toy company to Photoshop vibrators into Sad Girl Summer Starter Packs. In their email inviting me to speak on a conference panel, representatives of the narcissism app referred to all this as *an incredible career trajectory*.

When it first launched, the narcissism app was an externalized catalog of interiority, without the fussiness of language. It differed from other apps in its formal circumscription—square photographs, presented in reverse chronological order against a uniform white background—and in its fetishization of the analog. The point was to reference authenticity without committing to it. With your phone camera, you could create a digital facsimile of the kind of Polaroids you saw in a wooden box in the flea market, or in your parents' wedding album, or on the blogs of jewelry maker–musician husband-wife teams. In contrast to the reblog or the hundred-photo album, you were curating keepsakes: a fishbowl containing two live goldfish, left on the curb (2 likes); plastic wedding bands in the pod machine at the laundromat (6 likes); a pile of snow-dusted trash, glowing nightclub red in the lights of a nearby police car (0 likes).

It didn't matter that once externalized, interiority was kind of ugly. The narcissism app had filters. I already knew that beauty was less a quality than a skill. I knew the power of dancing at half-tempo in a crowded bar to evoke a dreamlike, languid femininity, and how you could forge a lifetime friendship overnight if you bought terrible battery acid cocaine from Cameron the Williamsburg Sheraton concierge and snorted it until your vulnerabilities had hardened into coinage and then exchanged those anecdotes of childhood trauma and personal failings until dawn clawed gingivitis pink at the skyline, jittery confidants, business partners in the economy of personal suffering.

THE MUSEUM OF WHO I WANT TO BE FOR YOU

To post was to work directly in the medium of desire. It was easy to take the new verbiage of *engagement* at face value: the idea that my *self*, at any given time, was less a static thing than a series of interactions with the world. To post a photo on the narcissism app was to be in relation with whoever might view it: materializing in front of them and asking them to reach out, with their soft warm hands, and touch the tiny heart next to your face. I had seized the means of production of my own image, I told myself, augmenting the vignette and the Valencia filter to a photo of my face in profile, eating a french fry not *not* in the style of someone licking a penis (8 likes). To post was also to challenge what it meant to have something worth keeping. It was a joke—the offhand framing, the faux-serious expression—and a promise: our lives were worth archiving. My need to be liked was worth archiving.

Later I told people that the wily, self-effacing performance of interior monologue was a side effect of fourth-wave feminism, a rejoinder to the glossy beauties who overtook one's feed to lip-synch and bake sourdough bread. Privately, being extremely online felt more akin to a sort of emotional girlfriend experience, but instead of the girlfriend, I was the supporting actor, the lovable fuck-up: clever but not threatening. Just someone who moves the plot forward. Maybe it was one response to a childhood of watching hidden-camera television shows, the messaging of which was, *Look how bad we are when no one is looking.* Spritz an unsuspecting mall walker with tuna water and tell her it's Chanel's latest, and she'll tell the camera it smells great. Drop a wallet and the finder will pilfer its contents. Without the moralizing gaze of the audience, people were selfish, embarrassing, gross, and cruel. People crave relatability, but not accountability. The performance of unwellness can be a catharsis for the artist and an act of service to the audience. I can hold your hand and assure you, *I am exactly as bad as you think I am.*

The last thing I'll say about memes is that it's strange, in this day and age, to have anything of indeterminate value. We're obsessed with haggling, negotiating, quantifying, listing, challenging, buying, selling. What's a meme worth? Nothing and something. For the meme conference, I was paid three thousand dollars, plus a travel stipend, to speak for ten minutes.

The narcissism app's New York offices were in a bank building, an anonymous behemoth of stone and steel and pigeon spikes and reflective windows, so whatever pigeons weren't deterred by the spikes flew headlong into a wall of sky and died on impact. Inside, at a long and imposing security desk, I handed over my driver's license and proof of vaccination in exchange for a collection of laminated badges on a lanyard, and then was I herded toward my fellow promising young memers.

The first internet person I ever met in real life was a basement hardcore musician named Cole who also made, in his words, *stupid stuff for attention.* Cole messaged me to ask if I lived in LA because he'd just moved there, and I did, so he asked if I could pierce his nose with a safety pin. It was fine until I hit the cartilage. I hadn't expected so much resistance and so I balked, which twisted the pin. Cole jerked back like a biblical dragon with an arrow in its heart. The safety pin fluttered. He turned away from me and pushed it all the way through to the hollow of his nostril and then pulled it out, and I held a fist of toilet paper to his face until the blood was stanched and he pushed an Icing by Claire's hoop earring through the hole. After that Cole sent me the occasional furtively horny text, but we never hung out again. Last I heard he moved to Atlanta and got canceled for dating an edgelord e-girl who turned out to be a nazi e-girl.

My meme conference co-panelists were a taurine former high school athlete named Lucas who performed one-man sketches and a woman named Victoria who ate vast quantities of noodles while dissecting her Tinder dates, and it was funny because she ate so many noodles and was still so thin. What united us was our valiant pivot to video. Lucas and Victoria were not former hobbyists with mental illness; theirs was a premeditated fame. They'd intentionally turned to the internet to make money. Did everyone think I made money? The three of us fiddled with our embarrassment of security badges and discussed audience growth until a team of blandly handsome employees arrived to escort us upstairs.

What we saw of the office was lit brightly as a laboratory, pocked with faux-suede sofas and clusters of beanbags. It reminded me of the platforms for the shuttles that take you between terminals at the airport. Like something was moving behind the walls. You could be whisked away at any time—which wasn't true, of course, considering the security rites we'd performed to get there. One of our escorts magnanimously informed us that we could take anything we wanted from the snack station, a sort of open-air kitchenette with salted almonds and power bars and CBD sodas. I panickily hovered over the snacks before grabbing what turned out to be a plastic pouch of bone broth. Too self-conscious to hold everyone up by using the microwave, I sucked the room-temperature broth like a baby as our hosts led us to the conference room.

I wanted the employees of the narcissism app to be shellacked and shark-like, nonchalantly evil sorcerers who tapped a mainline of unease between their algorithm and my brain. If those people do exist, they surely exist at companies like the one that hired me to speak—but the employees I met were self-deprecating, if not downright apologetic, about their line of work. Maybe they were posturing for my benefit; maybe I wasn't important enough to merit the presence of a real sociopath. They acknowledged how silly the conference was and, in the same breath, how exciting.

The conference was invitation-only, hand-selected by the meme liaison department. Every attendee, it was understood, had the dual goals of audience growth and brand endorsements. There was no abashed examination of the motives behind one's compulsion to post; the conference was less concerned with *why* than *how*. How do you gain followers fast? How do you monetize? How do you make it?

A few months before I first downloaded the narcissism app, I enrolled in an analog photography class. The plan was to force my way into conversation with the photographer Francesca Woodman. I'd gone to her retrospective at the Guggenheim and fallen in love with her casual self-obsession, the way she centered and then obliterated herself. A pane of glass pressed against her face, distorting it; a plastic tarp blurred her body as she stood stock-still in the corner of her haunted house. I loved the way she looked in motion in a still room. She turned, she tilted. Behind her, a window.

That art and self were entwined felt obvious to me, or at least convenient. I believed Socrates's assertion that we might achieve virtue if we studied ourselves hard enough, and if Socrates had been condemned to drink hemlock for corrupting the ancient youth, that made his philosophy all the more credible. I photographed myself over and over again, from different angles, my face grainy and obscured. I covertly recorded my conversations with people and listened back to them, searching for the moment we shifted course because someone answered a different question from what was asked. I was always sick with hangovers and allergies and once walking pneumonia, and I was amazed at how I could be in and then out of myself: my body, endlessly producing mucus, a bog where my soul should be. I pressed my used tissues in polyethylene document sleeves. In a yellow hard-covered journal that I was always losing and finding, I listed trash I saw in the street: *Two empty medical gloves, white latex, rolled inside out and the inside is smooth like the belly of a fish. A mysterious brown bag next to some cigarette butts. I don't know what's in the bag, it could be a balloon, it could be a sandwich.* Life was a series of formal decisions: whether I took my medication that day, or bought coffee instead of catching the bus, or texted some guy from some bar eight times in a row. The self was a tool that allowed me to access the world, or to reject it—to distance myself by creating new realities rather than participate in the one laid out for me, with its smelly sidewalks and overpriced cereal and indifference to who lives a good life and who does not. I knew that brilliance was a white deer in the dark forest of mundane existence, a flash from beyond the tree line. I just needed to look harder.

Unfortunately, negotiating the mundane required a vast internal catalog of train times and pharmaceutical dosages and knowing which contacts in your phone were vague because they were from OkCupid and which were vague because they were drug dealers, and the catalog required near-constant updates. Everyone else seemed able to affirm their identities with internships and BuzzFeed quizzes. **We Know What You're Thinking When You Look Out the Window Based on Which Dog Shares Your Aura. Make a Breakfast Plate and We'll Tell You When You're Going to Die.** Was this how it went, in the missing movie scenes? Other people showed up to class. They flossed. They blogged. My artist friends were always *in process*. Gretchen was unlearning her body through movement. Cloud shattered amethyst crystals with a rubber mallet and then encased the shards in concrete to destabilize space and form. Milo painted, maybe, but more importantly, Milo was in the hot tub of an up-and-coming video artist or en route to Art Basel with some silver-haired collector. Milo's ability to draw power from objectification was another reason I admired him; he understood the end goal, which was the highest bidder.

It was hard not to look at Francesca Woodman's photographs and see her casting herself out of them. At the Guggenheim, she looked into my eyes the moment before the chair tipped back. You could go to a jewelry shop in Chinatown and have a photo of your aura taken. You put each hand on a large brass box and looked straight ahead, and then a pop and a flash and the shop owner handed you a paper cup of tea and a Polaroid with flares of red and limpid swirls of blue around your head, a gauzy halo. This was what it meant, I thought, to photograph the future. Of course I thought that: My phone didn't yet have a backward-facing camera, a way to look ahead and only see myself.

Victoria, Lucas, and I sat on a spotless white sofa on a kidney-shaped stage. In front of us were three hundred empty chairs. The wall-to-wall screens behind us were off, but they reflected the blue carpet, so it felt like we were in someone's aquarium.

There was something sweetly sad about our moderator; he was likable in the basset hound way. He wanted us to succeed. He shuffled his notecards.

How did you pivot to full-time content creation?

"I hated my marketing job," said Victoria. "I feel so much freer marketing myself."

Where do you find inspiration for your comedy?

"I take all my jokes from Tumblr," said Lucas. "It's like someone already audience-tested them for you."

What were you really scared of when you first started?

Not long before the conference, I'd driven through the desert to visit a friend in Arizona. The land was flat and pink and rippled toward some mountain range I didn't know the name of.

The highway was under construction, a string of concrete barriers erected on either side of the two lanes. *The light is beautiful*, I thought as I drove, and, *The road is getting narrower.* Realization passed over me like the shadow of a bird flying overhead: I knew the road wasn't getting narrower. A truck was sliding from the right lane into mine. It veered smoothly toward me, and I hit the gas, and my sensible Subaru sped up but not fast enough, and the concrete barrier was to my right and the truck was to my left and also in front of me, the gas pedal, the horn, I saw the narrowing desert horizon and the rivets on the truck's side panels—how did I see the rivets, sometimes I still see them—and then the barrier ended and I was shot out into the clear desert and swerved and honked again and out of the bottleneck, one shaking middle finger to the sky, I was alive.

I should have felt relief, and I did—but I couldn't shake that I had been so close. That's how I felt all the time. A life of unhappiness and failure had pressed into me, and by some brute chance, some flash of luck or fate, I had swerved. I made it, and I was still afraid.

"Learning Adobe Suite," I said.

Victoria and Lucas had never been to New York before, so they asked if I would walk them back to the hotel.

"It's this way," I said.

"Believe women," said Lucas.

I walked us back and my memers followed behind me, phones out. Was that taxi funny? Was that homeless man? I felt jealous;

when I took out my phone, I imagined someone else filming me filming things, putting it on the internet: **Bad artist begs for engagement!!** We walked past the college, the classrooms I'd failed out of and the bars I'd been thrown out of. I didn't say any of this to Victoria and Lucas. They were discussing their NYC content, boosting engagement, maybe they could collab. They could eat bagels, or say *Ay! I'm walkin' here!* In some ways, the internet feels like a neutral energy in the way that money is a neutral energy, only as virtuous or wicked as the person using it. But then you have to follow that line of inquiry somewhere annoying, like *Am I using it for good?*

We stopped at a light, and a small dog on a leash trotted past us. "Look," I pointed, "one of those famous New York rats."

"That's really good," said Victoria. She and Lucas raised their phones with the grace of synchronized swimmers. "Look," they took turns saying into their respective phone cameras, alternating so each could be heard, and each got a clear shot of the dog. "One of those famous New York City rats."

I read somewhere that it's a function of human neurological development to walk into a room and forget why you entered it—it's the doorway, and the passage through it, that causes the forgetting. Your brain responds to the threshold. More and more, the narcissism app felt like a doorway. The nanosecond of blank screen as it loaded: a memory cleanse.

With film photography, I was stuck in the world of the photograph, even when I was out of frame. I hated that I couldn't disappear. The camera would click and I would still be there, and then I'd have to answer for why I wanted to capture the lovers on the Brooklyn-bound M or the drunk man scruffing the bodega cat or the daisy chain of children whipping across traffic, led by a caustically silent nun. What did I want from them? I was throwing a net into a dark sea, hoping to pull up some object—shivering in the moonlight—that would expose my life's great meaning. Pulled slick from wet bins of fixer, my exposures revealed none of this. I couldn't make anything look real. The flatness of my work was almost trippy, in an uncanny valley way; it suggested that the artist had never once encountered a human interaction. My grades were middling. My professor's criticism, invariably, was that my photographs looked like they were trying to sell something.

The morning of the conference, I woke early, my bodily impulses firing before my brain caught up. By the time I breached consciousness—clocked the dim sunrise, wondered when someone last mopped the floor I was kneeling on—I was already hunched over the toilet, heaving silky bile into the porcelain bowl. My skin burned. I gulped for air, stripped off my T-shirt, haphazardly attempted a bun but didn't quite make it before gagging again. I thought, *My body is resisting consumption.*

At the app's headquarters I was once again screened, tagged, and escorted upstairs. The warren of white tables and potted plants and vaguely appropriative graffiti-inspired art was now teeming with content creators. Outside the conference room, we engaged in the brute choreography of networking: a frisson of meeting and greeting, space buns and streetwear and that glazed-over apathetic approximation of interest, mouths curling with compliments, eyes flicking to the elevator bank. On a row of folding tables, someone had set up a spread of sweaty cheese cubes and vulvic folds of deli meat.

Like many people who spend a lot of time on the internet, real life interaction makes me anxious. The most adept internet personalities are actually great with people; they're at once radically self-centered and outward-facing, deftly navigating what is essentially a customer service job with a 24/7 suggestion box with an adroit ability to mete out the self. Portion control for the soul. It's not entirely untrue when the app tells us we're helping people. Whether people put themselves on the internet out of catharsis or narcissism, you can't be a mirror for the audience—which is to say, relatable—without losing a bit of yourself. In some ways, then, you could argue it's selfless.

The other side of this, however, is that in real life you end up giving delicate half-hugs to a hundred people who aren't all there. Presence wasn't the purpose of the conference, of course. The objective of an event like this wasn't intimacy. It was amplification. It was a training seminar; the narcissism app was better preparing us to sell ourselves. We reaped our benefits in the form of engagement and, perhaps, if we were lucky, the occasional sponsorship. The app, in turn, won views, data, money, and stock value—whether we succeed or not. The point was not to have ten thousand success stories, but ten thousand users striving for success. I—the panelist—was the middleman between the consumer and the app, and I was also the consumer, and also the product, and the other consumers were also the product, too. The only one that wasn't the product was the narcissism app, which coincidentally marketed itself as the product.

Overeager the day before, the conference's organizers were now hyperreal with enthusiasm. Guiding me to the sound technicians, one woman told me she loved how fucked-up I came off, and she seemed to really mean it. Another revealed that I was her "goal weight." "Not *too* thin," she said.

The room was a glowing cube, the stage lights fitted with blue and purple gels so light pooled in the grooves of the carpet. The hanging screens behind the white sofa were ablaze with orange graphics, corporate logos swirling. Along one wall, organizers paced and whispered into earpieces and arranged VR headsets on a folding table. I mournfully informed the sound guy I didn't have a bra strap on which to pin his lavalier microphone, so we ended up clipping it to a chunk of my hair. Creators streamed into the room, and the conference began.

A pretaped sequence performed by narcissism app ambassadors played on the giant unseeing screens. The ambassadors were transported to a universe of memes via virtual reality. Actually, a lot of the conversation veered toward virtual reality—specifically, the virtual reality project currently in beta at the narcissism app. Activities included a magic show I didn't experience firsthand but witnessed via a twentysomething man in a black tracksuit who twitched at one of the tables until he got dizzy. There was a *Caption This Photo* game and an NFT panel in which an edge of defensiveness never left the moderator's voice. Words like *community* and *empowerment* were bandied about. And then they cued us, and my comrades and I sat on the white sofa, and one of my own videos flashed on-screen. The camera operators, clad in black and trailed by ropes of tangled cordage, swept their large black lenses onto us.

Most of my friends from the internet weren't invited to the meme conference. They'd been deemed unpalatable—overly sexual or anarchist, or maybe they'd buckled under the pressure to produce, the anxiety of surveillance, and the lack of material reward. They talked about actual problems, the ugly kind. I, on the other hand, was a featured guest because my brain disorder was safe. It was the skinny Oreo to their full-fat crème experience: guilt-free. Some microcelebrities publicly spiraled and were then derided for their inability to adhere to the script; others were rewarded for what the audience saw as a performance of mental illness instead of a legitimate crisis. Some overdosed or died by suicide. Some lived but died a thousand little times posting GoFundMes over and over again, which isn't at all inherently bad, but at some point people start asking *Shouldn't somebody else be paying you?* (And yes, but who—whose job is that? Whose job is ours?) Others simply deactivated one day and never returned. I attended Zoom funerals, reposted Cash App codes, went to the meme conference and told the audience they could have what I have and more. They just had to want it. Milo, with his beautiful hands, swerved his moped into a passenger van in Greece. Because I didn't follow him, he'd been gone a year before I learned he'd died.

Offstage, I was informed that I had slayed. I said, half-honestly, that I had blacked the whole thing out.

"Dissociation!" trilled a handler with a tight ponytail and a jangle of friendship bracelets. "If we didn't have drug tests, I'd be on ketamine all the time."

The staff took us to the corporate gelato bar for ice cream and gifted us each a mug with a hashtag on it. I shook hands, grinned, tried to temper a nervous flush.

"It was really beautiful, what you said about making memes for mental health," a man who curated content for four million followers told me at the elevators. At last year's digital conference, the app's creator had personally thanked him for his service. In real life the man was fortysomething, bald, and buff in the way men who lose their hair early often are; he looked like he should be barking criticism from the sidelines of a soccer field.

"Yeah," I said. And then, because we were sort of on the subject, "But it's weird with you know…the horrors."

"I'm glad to get to choose the best thing," the creator said. "You don't want options? You want only one toothpaste? One newspaper?" I'd treaded wrong somewhere. I'd heard of this argument, trotted out by Thanksgiving uncles, but usually the argument was against communism. Also, didn't a billionaire buy *The Washington Post*? I felt clammy in the vintage mechanic's jumpsuit I'd originally chosen because it freed me from the burden of matching two disparate clothing items, but now felt smugly faux proletariat. I suspected there was still vomit in my hair.

"I guess," I said.

The elevator dinged. He looked past me, down the antiseptic hallway. "I just..." He trailed off. "I have to believe it's good. I have to believe that."

I skipped creator karaoke. I ordered sushi and a bottle of wine to go and watched the hostess sing quietly along to a J-pop ballad while she tied the plastic bag handles into a bow for me.

In addition to mirrors, the hotel offered something called an Essentials Room that had a machine that sold condoms, Android chargers, and Advil; three ironing boards and irons; and an ice machine. I tried to angle the hotel-provided water carafe, shaped like a farmhouse milk jug and entirely useless, under the ice machine. The machine was programmed somewhere between cube and pellet and shot ragged chunks around the Essentials Room. The carafe was small, unaccustomed to violence. When pellets of ice hitting my face started to bore me, I put it under the jet of water, and then I left the Essentials Room and walked back down the hallway to my room.

In my room, I flipped to whatever channel plays *Law and Order* on loop in hotel rooms and ate in bed. On a photo forum, I hunted for content. I scrolled through animals doing things and tried to find one that looked like how I felt: a baby hippo biting a booted calf; a bear climbing a tree. In the hotel room the sheets were like any hotel sheets. The windows didn't open. The ice had melted. A stroke on the text, a stamp filter, median blur. A self-portrait. Attention so pure you could snort it. I checked to see which of my fellow panelists had posted my rat joke, and I wasn't even in the background.

The most authentic photograph I ever posted was taken at a house party, after the beer but before the trauma swap. It's a digital photo of a Polaroid, posted one month before the first ever sponsored post—for Michael Kors—appeared on the narcissism app.

In the photograph, I look into the camera. My bangs are bleached blond and fluffy and my eyes are large and dark and my cat eyeliner is uneven in just the right way. I'm wearing a black button-down dress from Forever 21 that I cut into a jagged mini with children's craft scissors, a dog collar, and sheer black pull-up stockings. You can see the oil-slick quality of the Polaroid film in the light, the distorted reflection of my phone hovering above it to photograph it. My headed is tilted, my lips slightly pursed; I'm listening to someone out of frame.

It could have been any party. Any rooftop, any bar with no sign outside and a bartender who calls you by name. It could have been a night where I cried or threw up into the sleeve of my sweater or woke up among the ruins of a mysteriously acquired bodega sandwich, lettuce strewn across my bedroom floor like frilly panties. It could have been the party where, out of frame, Milo told me the secret of the highest bidder. The highest bidder did not want to display Milo's art. Art was nothing but capital. The collector's goal, and thus Milo's goal, was to purchase his work and then keep it in storage on the gamble that it would eventually accrue value. The dream, Milo told me, was temperature control.

I don't know who took the most authentic photograph of me, but looking at my face, I know what I was thinking. I was thinking, *It will be so fun to tell someone about this.* I look happy.

I get up early and check out of the hotel on one of the iPads. Someone has repaired the escalators. I descend in my cloud of gold, infinitely, just standing there. I order an Uber on my phone and, conveniently, a gig worker is dispatched to collect me.

On the plane, I apply moisturizer. I writhe around in my neck pillow and strap my wrist into a carpal tunnel brace and smear the permagrease around the lenses of my reading glasses with a soft cloth. I'm getting older. And then I am in the air, in emptiness, picking up speed, rising to heights at which the human body cannot breathe.

HOW TO DO THE RIGHT THING

"ARE YOU GOING to cancel me?" Adam has the sort of bland, dispassionate face onto which you could project almost any emotion, but when he looks scared—as he does now, leaning against a jacaranda tree—he's lit from within in a way you've never seen before. The vulnerability is jarring. He is radiant with helplessness, and something like pleasure flashes through you, and then something like disgust.

Adam is neither ugly nor handsome. He's a self-reported six feet tall, with moderate rosacea and the budding neck hump of the extremely online. He sends you sweaty selfies from his jogs around the Silver Lake Reservoir, but his body has a sort of resigned softness to it, like an old cardboard box. He was born to Nordic Midwesterners in a town that is neither urban nor rural. His parents are kind, you've heard, but intellectually stunted; he hates the gentle bovine look in their eyes when he explains his art to them. Adam's art is anti-comedy comedy posters that say things like *Soak in my broth*, which he staples to street signs, photographs, and posts on Instagram as if he stumbled upon them. Adam's eyes are brown, probably. He rarely makes eye contact. He's self-conscious about his strabismus. Adam is the neurotic brand of comedic genius, prone to bouts of depression and anxiety, awkward around girls. Which is how you got here.

August in Los Angeles is a month of foreshadowing. The heatwave breaks in September: the river dries to a crust of garbage and the air takes on a chalky quality, as if permeated with ash, which it is sometimes, if the first seasonal wildfire has sparked. August is dazzling toothy sunshine, but portentous—holding the summer's heat in its hands before unleashing it on you.

The day cools and you and Adam amble through the watery dusk, past patchy yards punctuated with statues of gnomes and saints and the flags of real and imagined nations, stucco bungalows, gentrified neo-craftsmen that sport the same silver house numbers straight from the millennial minimalism factory. You've come from work, your clothes stained with coffee and printer ink, your shoes practical. You tapped blush across the bridge of your nose before he arrived, and now that you're walking, you loathe yourself for it.

You've pored over infographics on community justice in a carceral world, sat in church basements and therapists' offices and considered the question of redemption. You don't feel prepared. The infographics were static, the meetings over in an hour; there was no mention of what happens outside the post, on the sidewalk, at the fuzzy edges of discourse.

You shake your head. "Have you thought about it, though? A little?"

The neighborhood used to have a butterfly season. Monarchs would flutter through on their southern migration, thousands of them. They surfed invisible currents and got chased by stray cats, propelled through the quiet streets by some unknowable impulse. *This is the way.* The monarch population has been decimated by pesticides, though, so now you see only a few per year, if you're lucky.

"I'm just shocked." Adam shakes his head. "I never thought this would happen to me."

"I mean about her."

"Well…" Adam studies the gutter. "I remember a few elements of the story differently." You open your mouth, and he hurries to add, "But I've realized that doesn't matter, because ultimately her story is reflective of how I made her feel. I understood the situation to be positive and mutual, and I was clearly not being as perceptive as I thought." He looks to you for affirmation.

"Perceptive about…" You trail off, and he lets you, until you answer the question for both of you, "Consent."

He nods, once. "In the future, I need to read less into body language, and do a better job of seeking verbal enthusiastic consent." The words are there, but there's something about his tone—a resigned precision, like he's splitting a check six ways after dinner. Or like he's reading words off a teleprompter. Does that make you the live audience, or the scrolling text?

* * *

HOW TO DO THE RIGHT THING

One week earlier, the screenshot had wafted in on whatever shitpost zephyr powers the windmill of your Instagram feed. Pet photo, GoFundMe, Drake meme, communist infographic, thirst trap, sympathy trap, mental health infographic, lizard in a tiny vest, screenshot. You were on your back on your lumpy unmade bed, your phone held precariously aloft like you were blessing and threatening yourself at the same time.

We know the internet flattens information, presenting data to you all-you-can-eat and demanding that you digest a photo of a blurry moon and a photo of a dead child with the same metabolic rigor. But humans are designed to adapt. We soften our focus, temper our frontal lobes, quell the amygdala firing its warning shots. If not for the bright purple **UMMMMMMM** splashed across what looked like any other jumble of photo and text, you might have flicked past the screenshot. You saw purple, and then you saw Adam's face.

Two photos: one you recognized from his Instagram, and a foreign one in which he was wearing a cowboy hat and holding his tabby cat, Trader Joe, who was also wearing a cowboy hat. The framing, the buttons: a Tinder profile. *I didn't know he was on Tinder* whipped through your head, unbidden, before you read the text. The screenshot was a Facebook post, and the Facebook post was a screenshot of Adam's Tinder profile, and the text alongside it read

WATCH OUT this boy does not care about consent!!!

met this guy on tinder and we went to my apartment after drinks. we made out and i said i wanted things to stay PG, but despite this he tried to put his dick in me over and over again. i told him i didn't want to have sex but he would not listen, to the point where i pushed him away and said he could deal w blue balls and tried to throw him out. he proceeded to jerk off on my bed. no means no!!!

People always say things like *time stopped*. The truth is, you stopped. You pressed your thumb to the phone screen to keep the screenshot from disappearing as time sped on around you. The blood in your ears whispered *nonononono*. The story was a tiny self-destructing bomb. Every second ate away at its lifespan. You could lift your finger, if you wanted. It would be the lightest, smallest motion, that release. You could watch the story float by like nothing ever happened, let the molten core of what no longer happened melt away your insides.

You screenshotted the screenshot and sent it to Adam.

> **YOU**: hey i don't mean to freak you out but have you seen this
> **ADAM**: whoaa this is highly upsetting :((
> **YOU**: i mean did that happen?

You hate scenic vistas because it's impossible not to think about flinging yourself off them. Some small part of you wants, more than anything, to know that terrible anticipation as the earth rises up to meet you. The vertiginous space between question and answer. did that happen? hovered above your face like some terrible specter. A froth of ellipses: Typing. Nothing. Typing. Nothing.

When Adam first followed you on Instagram, he had twenty-two thousand followers and you were superimposing self-deprecating jokes over pirated pictures of Bobby Hill for an audience of twelve hundred. You taught yourself bootlegged Photoshop in the smelly fluorescent production office of a documentary television show about the beauty of the universe. Whirling galaxies and gauzy eddies of stars, the miracles of life and the mysteries of death, et cetera. Programming oriented toward stoned millennials looking for a quirky date night watch. You were a production assistant, still are. The physics are always just out of reach—you could read a million scripts and not quite understand antigravity—but you love the collision of comets, the quivering migrations of planets, and the impossible fact of heavenly bodies, heavy and hostile, suspended in their tense negotiations with gravity.

On earth, you watch the sunset on other people's Instagram stories. You collate scripts and validate parking and send endless emails explaining how one might connect to the printer. You haggle over steaming trays of rice to feed the crew, which they'll complain about anyway. You chauffeur bistro soups and seasonal salads to the showrunner and her twitchy mustached nephew, who inherited a producer title and flexes it by hovering near your desk and saying you should get drinks sometime. The showrunner's nephew isn't as bad as the visual effects producer who asked you to print a sign for his office door that says *Anti Me Too Department*, or the executive who berates you for infractions he just invented and calls one-on-one emergency meetings in which he falsely promises you a pay bump in exchange for executing some convoluted task, such as coding a journal-spreadsheet hybrid with an algorithm for sorting action items, or booking an esthetician to come wax everyone's brows. This is normal. This is putting in your time.

The job is a paradox: You are profoundly important and profoundly replaceable. Lose a receipt, distribute the wrong draft, rebuff the showrunner's nephew's flaccid advances—*You'll never work in this town again!* Scribbling down money-squandering ideas or loading paper into the bitchy printer, you sometimes feel like you're electrically wiring a dollhouse: the scale of the task is minuscule, but if you fuck up, the shock is life-sized. The closest you get to stars and satellites is when you track the sun's celestial journey across the smog-fuzzed office windows during your twelve-point-five-hour shifts.

For all your abjection, though, you might have the firmest grasp out of anyone when it comes to alternate dimensions. In the liminal space between menial tasks, you log on to Instagram and talk with your invisible friends about your boring day jobs, your horoscopes, your crushes and breakups and parents' divorces. The way you see it, self-destructive sorrow had always belonged to men: Ernest Hemingway and Vincent van Gogh, David Foster Wallace and Conor Oberst. Women were the catalysts for sorrow but rarely the blameless victims of it; the failures of women were domestic, embarrassing, narcissistic. Billie Holiday was a junkie, Mama Cass was fat, Britney Spears a psycho, Marguerite Duras a drunk. Their sadness made them less likable, not more. With the internet, though, girls and their allies had found a loophole. If you could hold sorrow at arm's length—if you could philosophize it or, better yet, deprecate it—you could transmute it into something worthy of public consumption.

This alchemy existed before the internet, but in secret. You found it in bathrooms and on ratty sofas and in the peeling booths of low-lit wine bars, women talking while sucking the meat from oily olives and depositing the pits into a tiny artisan-crafted ceramic dish. The internet amplified those whispers, stripped them of shame, and added a laugh track. *And then they said they wouldn't take my insurance hahaha my body is a joke my job's a joke my abortion my psychiatrist my father lol I think I'm afraid of everything and I'm responding to the world from this place of horny fear lmao do they still make Smirnoff Ice let's reclaim Smirnoff Ice lol my friend's brother bought it for us once and I threw up in a creek bed haha is that littering if it's organic material lol my friend's brother patted my back then pushed his hand up my shirt ha there was still vomit on my chin ha what an asshole I'm okay though lmfaoooo.* You think maybe the only way to talk about anything is to circle it, laughing, like a hyena closing in on its prey.

Your obsession with Instagram—the bloom of pride you feel when someone follows you; the parasocial semi-erotic friendships with leggy sad women across the world, built on the thin framework of late-night DMs and shared psychiatric history—is mortifying. Publicly demanding the attention of strangers horrifies you, but you can't stop doing it.

When Adam followed you, and then suggested drinks, you were mostly excited to openly indulge in your dirty secret—to speak candidly of seeking attention. Maybe he'd post a picture of you together. You barely dared to want it.

You didn't know your first date with Adam was a date. You'd kind of assumed he was gay, because everyone on Instagram was gay, and he had a T-shirt that read *Males "R" Canceled* in the Toys "R" Us font and he regularly posted about how grateful he was to support the trans artist who made it. He loved his cat. He heart-eyes reacted your Instagram story about Agnès Varda. At any rate, you were meeting up to talk about the internet. With your twelve hundred followers, you wondered if the internet could be a way out of your life—not just in the scrolling-during-lunch way, but as something more permanent. Of all the television assistants you knew, only two went on to write for their respective shows, and both had assisted for seven years. Seven years of smiling and showing up early and getting chewed out for things you didn't do by people you didn't respect—you didn't have seven years in you. But people were plucked from the social media masses all the time, offered representation and a seat in a writers' room and a future.

You met at a dive bar with goth décor and cheap tequila and you paid for your own drink. On the patio, Adam watched the table of girls behind you as he spoke of his posting schedule, his analytics, how his manager had found him *organically*. You sipped your tequila and nodded, made a mental note to google *analytics* when you got home. He'd gone to film school—USC, he mentioned several times, not the grad school but the undergrad program, which was also very acclaimed—and worked at a buzzy media startup, producing comedy shorts with a roster of talent you recognized by handle but not by name. It was fine, he said, but his real passion was interacting with his audience. You tried to picture twenty-two thousand people in a theater, or on the freeway. Twenty-two thousand monarch butterflies. At work, you were constantly marveling at the vastness of the universe: billions of light-years, billions of stars, a world bursting with flora and fauna and infinite mycelium networks. It turned out that it did not take a vast universe to induce awe in you. You could be taken in by far less.

"Your place is around here?" Adam sloshed the ice in his drink. He seemed bored. It was so embarrassing, how you fidgeted, how fast you drank, how desperate you were to fill space with talk, with motion—to rustle his quiet boredom into a human interaction. In the bar, as on the internet, you craved engagement.

You'd been drinking while he was talking; you were a little drunk; he would drive you home.

The rest of the night unfurled predictably, in retrospect, though in the moment you remember feeling surprised. Adam was like a betta fish in a tank, floating indifferently until it suddenly turned to charge the glass. The soft thrill of someone wanting you is almost as good as wanting, you know. It's almost good enough to ignore that you were drunk, but not so drunk as to not ask for a condom, and twenty minutes later you were not so drunk as to not notice that his mediocre Midwestern dick was condomless. Some soft alarm pinged in the back of your mind, a searchlight in fog. And then the moment passed, and other moments passed, and you didn't say anything.

You're used to the prosaic disappointments of dating men. What a time to grow up, the nineties, when little girls were taught gender equality and little boys were not. What a time to live on the internet, with its raging incels and clueless husbands getting deservedly roasted on Twitter for saying they love their wives in spite of their weight. The idiocy of men has been immortalized in romcoms and sitcoms and memes with a sort of cheeky resignation. You liked the tweet about the skater who wouldn't text back, the guitarist who'd give you a UTI, the socialist with jealousy issues. lol, you said. What difference was the film bro who lost his condom?

And so that gentle flare faded into the mist. It flickers only every now and then. Like when you see a screenshot from another universe—someone else's bedroom—on Instagram. And so, when you ask *i mean did that happen*, you know it's a stupid question. What you mean is, *Should I have been more empowered about the condom thing?* And then: *If I had been, would things have gone differently with the girl in the screenshot?*

You need something other than dead air. That void between question and answer. You type:

> **YOU:** (fwiw i've always felt safe and good and like my boundaries are being respected when we hook up)

Bubbles materialize and dissipate. The gap closes. You hit solid ground.

> ADAM: we did go on a tinder date and had a sexual experience, but i think i'm a pretty self-critical person and that's not how i would characterize what happened
>
> ADAM: but i don't want to invalidate how she feels and feel really bad if i made her feel this way
>
> ADAM: i know my emotions arent the priority in this situation but i'm still so shocked and confused
>
> ADAM: i value you and your presence in my life and i want to do whatever i can to keep that

And now, you and Adam are on a walk.

Between then and now, you've watched the internet swallow the screenshot whole. No one reposted it. No one came for him in his comments. At your suggestion, he'd texted an apology to the girl who'd made the Facebook post, but she never responded. (Should you have suggested that?) And now Adam is asking you to help him. He is going to therapy. He would never do that, but he also doesn't want to invalidate anyone. The sidewalk is littered with fallen jacaranda blossoms, sticky and vaguely embryonic. Across some chasm—on some other street, inside some sentence you haven't thought of yet—is justice. What does that look like?

You assumed it would be like that legal definition of porn: You can't define it, but you'll know it when you see it. You feel like you're inside a math problem, some absurd calculation for x.

In college, you'd spent one summer working on a radio project, a story about for-profit prisons and carceral justice in rural Vermont. You visited a small town with a restorative justice board, where conflicts and infractions were managed by a panel of accountability advocates. Justice was a contrite letter, or a mediated conversation, or reimbursement for damaged property. This type of accountability—interpersonal, solution-oriented—was both graceful and pragmatic; studies have shown restorative justice lowers rates of reoffense. The rehabilitated offenders, when you spoke with them, were like you: lost and unwell and prone to fucking up. Unlike you, however, they were versed in the language of apology.

You interviewed delinquent teens and adult inmates, polite men with close-cropped hair. You interviewed the families of men who had been bused out of state with no warning. The mothers offered you cigarettes and the children stamped their hands onto construction paper Father's Day cards. You interviewed the parents of a man who had been stabbed in the skull with a ski pole. It was a mistake, looking back. You were probably supposed to interview a victim of petty theft. The dead man's parents lived in a double-wide somewhere near a thicket of brambles; his mother was soaking what looked to you like hundreds of blueberries in the kitchen sink. The dead man's father sat at the kitchen table across from you. He was a hulking man, stooped with rage. He shook and spat at you. They would never get him back, their baby boy. He wanted you to tell them why. The dead man's mother wept the whole time. You asked your asinine interview questions—*What does justice mean to you?*—and you watched the dead man's mother's hands, how she pulled them out of the murky sink water and patted her face with them. Her wet hands trying to dry her wet face. *Tell me why,* his father begged, and all you said was *I'm sorry. I'm so sorry.* The tape was unusable.

You and Adam come to a yard with an iron fence and a shrieking puppy that tumbles back and forth along the railing as you pass it. The puppy is perfect, silky and plump and slightly pug-nosed. *Puppy central casting,* you think. Adam is talking about rap music. Is rap music the problem? "Their lyrics portray women in a very negative light, you know."

"That's valid," you say. You'd learned in a therapy group, years ago, that you couldn't argue with someone's emotions. How much therapy qualifies you to therapize others? You guess just enough to validate them.

You wonder—if you slip your fingers through the wrought iron—if the dog will bite you.

Adam says, "I think I need to be more present."

"More present." You're chasing logic like shapes in the clouds: rhetoric shifting, dissipating. There's something to say, some question that would conclude this conversation, this pilgrimage toward salvation. You are thinking about recidivism, and about blueberries. You say, "How have you learned from this experience?"

"Well." Adam watches a passing car, as if the passing car can hear you. "I just put this insane pressure on—you know—girls. And when I feel rejected, I spiral. I get in these self-esteem ruts and I'm just so hard on myself." You round back on your house, his car.

"Do you feel bad?"

He thinks. "It hasn't affected my engagement—which maybe says something about society. I feel bad about that." You stop at your front yard, and he keeps walking to his car. "But Janelle posted that meme that was, um…accidentally racist a few weeks ago, and she said there was nothing to do but let the negative attention pass and move forward. You just have to, you know… move forward."

People say things like *Let's take things from there*. And so you do, and then you realize you don't know where you're taking things. You're just holding things, looking around. The sky has darkened since you left home.

"I mean," you say, "do you feel bad that you hurt someone?"

He's barely an outline in the lampless night. "Yes," Adam says, "of course I do."

You've always been needy. You had like twenty security stuffed animals as a child. In middle school you visited a Shetland Sheepdog puppy in a pet store every week for months. The puppy was skittish and strange, and you watched him grow into a dog while the younger, more normal puppies found homes. You cried until your mom rescued the dog from his plexiglass prison. The dog turned out to be intensely afraid of everyone but you. He slunk around the house, cowering, until bedtime, when he curled in the uppermost corner of the bed so his fur brushed your face when he breathed. You never thought he was weak. You thought he had chosen you.

As an adult, you obsess. You triple text. You spend the hours before every party shaving your body and honing your anecdotes, calculating how to appear most worthy of love. You've heard your own mouth repeat the same joke twice because you didn't get a response the first time. The person you dated before Adam induced a blushing, panicky crush in you. You were nonspecifically together for two blissful, nauseating months of feigning nonchalance and willing your phone to vibrate, and when it finally did your phone became a dog shaking itself after a swim in the ocean, pure jubilant release. Then you ate psychedelic mushrooms together and he cried for six hours and you rubbed his back and put on *Moana* and made spaghetti. Your microwave could only hold one bowl at a time, so by the time the second bowl of sauced spaghetti got hot, the first bowl was cold again. You ate the cold bowl. It wasn't love, but it could have been.

The next time you saw him, he told you that he'd done a lot of thinking while crying and watching *Moana*. He realized you loved your dog too much (your real dog, not your phone, but maybe in retrospect he meant that too). You fetishized your pet's dependency on you. It was clear to him that you'd bring the same desperation to any serious relationship, and you were a great girl, but he didn't even want to stay friends.

The boy you almost loved told you this on the day of the nature documentary's production accountant's birthday party.

She'd invited you to a sing-along performance of *Grease* at the Hollywood Bowl, nonrefundable, with a plasticky satin jacket that said *Pink Ladies* on the back. You sat in a crowd of seventeen thousand singing "Hopelessly Devoted," and then you excused yourself to cry in the bathroom, and the bathroom was flooded with Pink Ladies. Pink Ladies everywhere, jerking at the paper towels and adjusting their sunglasses and complimenting one another's jackets. Our Ladies of Pink Sorrow. You were just one of so many.

Something calcified in you, in the bathroom of the Hollywood Bowl. You course corrected. To balance the recklessness of your desire, you've learned to pull back, to question your impulses. You sleep five hours a night and work thirteen hours a day and sit in traffic for three-point-five hours a day, not counting picking up lunch. You wear baggy clothes so the showrunner's nephew can't compliment you, though everyone in the office assumes it's because of body dysmorphia.

One might posit that Adam is a response to the smothering sadness of the cheap satin jacket. Since that first date that wasn't a date, you've fallen into a relationship that isn't a relationship. He kept texting you, and after work you kept showing up to the backhouse that smells like Old Spice and chips where he lives, and you've slipped in and out of each other's lives like this until the in and out created a pattern, a running stitch.

He's like a daisy game: He texts you when he's feeling depressed (likes you) and calls your writing *a good start* (likes you not) and texts you first 99 percent of the time (likes you) and stops texting first 80 percent of the time (likes you not). He says things like "You're my favorite person to talk to" (likes you) and "It's funny that your parents aren't more ashamed of you for not graduating from college" (likes you not). He has a habit of pulling out his phone mid-conversation with you, dropping off to scan it no matter if it's you or him that was talking, with the unselfconscious ease of changing a television channel. But then there are strange bursts of affection—he wants your opinion on everything; he confides in you when he's sad. He pulls you in for a hug and it feels like touching your bare feet to a tile floor. You read somewhere that social media algorithms are modeled after the programming in slot machines, and Adam is a little like that too, doling out warmth and apathy at random.

There's safety in his simple entitlement—a buffer between you and the big sad world. You're one of the only people who knows how badly Adam wants to be rich and famous. He approaches his novelty sign making with comical gravitas, filling a whiteboard calendar with a rigid schedule of content production and monetization. He pays million-follower Instagram accounts twenty-five dollars a pop to repost his work, and anonymously shares his own account to Reddit with headlines like check out this guy, so funny. He is in secret Facebook groups devoted to the exchange of stock images. He tells you stories about your mutuals, and each anecdote feels like a party you weren't invited to. He disdains day jobs—he hasn't worked one in months, but his parents still believe he works at the media startup. When they call, he fabricates stories about his days in the office he no longer works in. It won't matter when he catches his break.

It's thrilling, Adam's expectation that great things are overdue for him. Fame is the prize for being a good boy, with his whiteboard schedule and his week of no carbs. You are entranced by his ability to wake up every day and bravely out-jog mediocrity. Solipsism can be a kind of optimism; to believe you matter is to believe *something* matters, after all. Is there such a thing as admiration without disdain? There it is: the evil smugness of knowing you have settled, just a little. Maybe you're the manipulator after all.

You'd shown your hand, once. Months ago, in May, during jasmine season. The air was heavy with love. You'd gone with a friend's friends to a kitschy Sunset Boulevard strip club where you knew one of the dancers from Instagram and were a little in love with her. You drank tequila sodas and slid money onto the stage. An Arcade Fire song came on and the girl you sort of knew from the internet arched her back and your friend's friend turned to you and said, "I could do that, if it wasn't for the shame."

By the time Adam asked where you were, you were dead drunk. He was at the bowling-alley-slash-karaoke-bar, but he was heading to a party, if you could get there in time. You remember the neon bath of the entrance, the far-off calamity of pins falling. In the bathroom mirror, you were radiant with booze; it coated you like the glossy finish on a photograph. You snorted a bump of coke with his housemate, a frail e-girl who had once, in all sincerity, asked you what ICE was, and you slipped. You said, "I like him, but I can't read him. I don't know how he feels."

His housemate, in solidarity with girls in bathrooms everywhere, was duty-bound to say *Why wouldn't he? He should be so lucky. You're literally glowing.* She betrayed her oath. She just shrugged, and you knew you'd fucked up. You thought about the dancer's body and the man singing Jimmy Buffett in the annex of the bowling alley, his voice lifting to the mold stains on the drop ceiling. You had wanted too much from the night, from your life.

Outside the bowling alley, while Adam called an Uber on your phone, you realized with horror that he was completely sober. You had to keep it together until the party, where maybe you could level out. You took great pains to pronounce your words right, your mouth slipping over the shapes of them. It didn't seem possible that his housemate had told him what you'd said but when he looked at you, it was with an air of detached disgust. You'd worn an orchid pink spaghetti-strap bodysuit and pink silk pants and pink leather heeled sandals, and you were struggling to maintain awareness of your body in space. You were acutely aware of how stupid you looked. You had wanted to dress like a flower, but now—holding yourself up against a parking sign while pretending you weren't—you only projected wilting.

Life went on; you didn't talk for a while, and then you orbited back to one another on whatever quiet current pulls you through life. You could never think about that night again. It's like a white-hot thing, something you can't look at directly.

"I don't want to have sex tonight," you tell Adam. It's the first time you've seen him since your walk. It feels obvious, but you also feel a little bad, like you're punishing him. Are you punishing him? It's been a week since the walk, and he's been overly kind, and you've been avoiding him. There's some caginess, some frenetic energy inside you that makes you incapable of waiting out the half-life of redemption. You feel a bit like a godparent left with a child after the sudden tragic death of their parents: Abstractly you're in charge, but you have no idea what to do. No one who signs up for this kind of thing thinks it will actually happen.

You've read about the bystander effect and the deafening silence of the indifferent. You've been on the other side of the screen before, witnessed the fall of the disgraced politician, the creepy celebrity, and head pusher. The burn of righteous anger when you hit Unfollow feels like retribution in the way that getting a massage feels like exercise. Maybe you're doing this because you run in the same circles—Adam is a physical presence in your life, online and off. He will not disappear if you turn away. When you try, he is on your phone screen, reposted, replicated endlessly. Over the course of your relationship, you've watched his audience grow to forty, fifty, sixty thousand. You can't suspend object permanence for him. When you say you run in the same circles, you mean you're tethered to the same pole.

Anyway, Adam kisses you. You're on your massive beige sofa that used to belong to your parents. When you sit on it, you feel at sea. "I don't want to have sex tonight," you say.

"Okay," says Adam. Your roommate Emily is coming home soon. You adore Emily, with her lilting voice and halo of lemony hair and passion for geeky fantasy fiction. You spend weekends blending chia seeds into barely drinkable health smoothies and wording each other's emails. You're confidants, privy to each other's crushes and heartbreaks and horror stories. Emily once went on a few dates with a trust fund kid from Hinge who left behind his sweater, and you passed it back and forth between you, taking turns sniffing his delicately spiced rich-person detergent. You can't explain, then, why Emily has never met Adam. Why, when he tugs your hand and says, "Should we—" you think of sitting on the giant couch with him and Emily, and Emily's expression, and you say, "Okay," and then you're in your bedroom.

And when he says, "Is this okay," he's already pushing up your dress.

"Okay?" Is it? You established the boundary. He heard you. And also, his hands are moving around. *He knows when to stop*, you remind yourself, and *It's supposed to feel good*. You're slow to answer; you feel like you're running out of time for something. Your thoughts are thawing on the counter. His hands, you realize, are untethered from his mouth; there's no connection between his hands and his question, his hands and your answer. There's no connection between your body and your brain. You're struck with an image from the nature show: a lizard detaching its tail to evade a predator. Where's Emily?

You think of a lizard, and you think of the night you hate remembering. The Uber didn't take you to a party. It took you to Adam's house instead. *Where's the party?* you thought. *He was too embarrassed to take me to the party.* When he pulled your stumbling body down the uneven concrete driveway, you felt so ashamed that the unconsciousness descending upon you felt like a blessing. And later, in bursts of wakefulness—sunlight on water—his body on yours—you felt a little pain, and humiliation, and you were trying to sit up and trying not to vomit and trying to remember your name and he was holding your body and your body was an object floating in space, or in this moment being held still, jerking around a little. Your body was a flimsy rowboat bobbing on a dark sea.

The next morning, Adam bought you a breakfast sandwich—the only thing he ever bought for you. "Do you remember a lot about last night?" he'd asked, as you picked at the sandwich, and you'd burned with embarrassment. In your gut: roiling nausea and the conviction that this all had something to do with what you'd said in the bathroom of the bowling alley. And then Adam dropped you off at home, and you didn't really talk for a while.

This is what you think of when you're sorting through your thoughts, unwinding into nothing like a star unwinds into clouds of gemstone-studded gas: *There was never any party.* Your body, Adam's weight, his greedy jutting chafing your thighs, then and also now.

"Um…can we…stop…" you ask, because yes, of course he started fucking you. "Please," you say, and Adam pulls his uncondomed dick out of your body and your body is as still as an icy lake somewhere very far away and Adam looks somewhere through you, huffing, charging toward his finish line, and then he cums on your dress and he smiles.

~~HOW TO DO THE RIGHT THING~~
HOW TO DO THE RIGHT THING

There is a theory of the creation of our solar system called the Theia Impact or, more playfully, the Big Splash. The idea is that 4.5 billion years ago, the young planet Earth cruised the same orbit as a Mars-sized dwarf planet scientists posthumously named Theia. At some point—if you could say there were points in the silky void that was not yet the universe—the heavenly bodies collided, due to what your nature show elliptically refers to as *gravitational disturbances*. When you look up gravitational disturbances on YouTube, you find a few industrial goth songs and several videos that look like early aughts iTunes visualizer effects. You wonder if the universe is really like this: million-mile-long skeins of electricity that whip through the dark to jolt a planet light-years away.

That astronomical collision—the Theia Impact—shattered the smaller planet into a jumble of free-floating rocks and dust. Some of Theia's debris was absorbed into early Earth; the rest swirled and hardened into our moon. And so due to the nature of gravity, the moon is pulled toward the planet that smashed it, stole from it. The moon is doomed to circle what ruined it forever.

It's September. The heat is a sledgehammer. You have an alarm clock with a light that mimics sunrise and a wake-up sound that mimics the sound of birds. You rise with your digital sun and birds, your enchanted forest of one. You nudge your car forward in a line of other cars in the viscous morning light. There's a film over everything that reminds you of the fuzz on unbrushed teeth. Your steering wheel is sticky. Your brain is sticky. The clock was supposed to make waking up easier, but instead it's made you hate real birdsong, too.

You need a plan. If you have a plan, you have control. Your body has begun to feel like an Airbnb, that eerie quality of a foreign house staged to look like home. You feel stretched out—you're playing chubby bunny with misery, taking it until your lips crack, until you choke on it. What even happened? You don't know how to talk about it, and so you don't know how to tell him it was wrong.

Your nightmares are boring. Adam is in your bed and you say to him, *I didn't mean it. Fuck me. I love you.* Sometimes you wake up to birdsong, and sometimes you wake up and you're in his apartment, because you're still going to his apartment. You pick your way through the detritus of his bedroom floor and sit on the toilet turning a three-in-one shampoo bottle over and over in your hands like it's some ancient artifact. The crust on the cap is the only thing that could save your life, if you focus. If you can just think. And then you slip out and go to work and wait for things to make sense.

Adam texts you first and often. He is concerned with his mental health, his pitch meeting, Oliver Stone documentaries, the CIA's endorsement of Jackson Pollock.

> **ADAM:** felt suuper unnecessarily down today, trying to meet up with psychiatrist soon to try something new

HOW TO DO THE RIGHT THING

ADAM: i may be going through a bout of crippling depression but at least i'm on the front page of reddit haha
ADAM: Got my hairs cut today what you think 10/10 handsome?

Sometimes you follow him around Silver Lake while he staple-guns his fake posters to telephone poles. He lifts his phone to photograph them and you step out of the way. Hanging out with him is like watching a house fire on TV while getting burned with a cigarette. *The Immersive Accidental Rape Experience,* you think. When the federal judge is accused of raping his high school classmate, you send him the victim's testimony. He calls it *intense & powerful*. You think, *At least if he's doing this to me, that means he isn't doing it to someone else.*

The documentary show host's hotel is on a street with impossible parking. You don't want production to yell at you for trying to reimburse a valet ticket, so you bargain with the attendant to park in the empty car wash zone. You're dropping off an international phone, whatever that is.

The lead is known for his offbeat magnetism. He is towering and broad and warm, and everyone treats him like he came up with the whole idea of planets himself. When you meet him for the first and only time in the hotel lobby, you smile and ask how he's finding Los Angeles. You hand him the phone, and he grabs your wrist, jerking you toward him.

"What is this?" He holds your forearm aloft, turns it to better examine a tiny tattoo.

"Oh"—relief—"It's a paw print. I had a pet hedgehog."

The lead nods once, releases you, and walks back to the elevator bank. You drive back to the office.

> **ADAM:** Hey, I'm thinking of making a facebook post about the callout situation. I just want to tell you in advance because i know it's very overwhelming for you and i understand if you don't want to deal with it or me ever again. But to move forward from it i feel that i need to write a bit about what I've learned these past weeks.

You're in the production bullpen, so you go to the bathroom and sit on the toilet. Adam sends you his accountability statement. His accountability statement is bad. Like, shockingly so. I'm still trying to process it, he writes. Some details diverge from what I remember...it has cost me years-long friendships and job opportunities. I am hurting, but maybe it is right for me to hurt now.

There is the thinly veiled denial, and the self-pity, the assertion that he has already been overpunished—but something else sticks with you. He writes, I've had many conversations with the women in my life about being more present, communicative, and perceptive in these situations. He speaks of consulting *some female friends.* Something clenches in you, reading that, the shock of your private conversation brought into the public sphere. You didn't realize that you've been publicly accountable for him.

"It comes off a little...defensive," you tell him, later, after work. Part of you wants him to post it, in all its pathetic solipsistic glory. But then you think of the other girl, the horror of reading that about yourself on the internet. You're walking around the Silver Lake Reservoir, shivering in the dying heat. "Like, I know that you're processing—and that's great—but maybe you could center it more on her, and her feelings?"

You are *some female friends.* You are *the women in my life.* You don't know how to tell him to leave you out of this. *It's true, though,* you think. You've laundered his reputation. You're so tired.

"That's a good point," he says. "How would you phrase it?"

"I just mean I maybe wouldn't push back on her interpretation of events."

"Right," he says, "but how would you say that?"

He never ends up posting it, anyway.

In the production office parking lot, you climb into the back seat of your car and lie down for a little bit. Your whole life feels like one of those Scooby-Doo hallways where every door leads back to the same corridor. You're in a time loop, you and the monsters. You are pursuing and you are being pursued. The real evil entity, you think, is the hallway itself—how you don't know how to escape it. That boy who broke up with you before the *Grease* sing-along at the Hollywood Bowl was wrong. Right to dump you, but wrong in how he framed it. You didn't want the dog to depend on you. You wanted to be the dog.

When Adam suggests one more walk, you think this is it: He's going to apologize. The education is complete.

He doesn't apologize. He says, instead, that he is *not all in*. He needs to focus on the present. You don't ask what about you distracts him from the present. Can you get coffee sometime? Are you still in his corner? Adam wants you to know you've been amazing.

The thing about nature documentaries is that they're less about nature as in *wildlife*, and more about nature as in *the nature of things*. Behavior, character, sensibilities. Many of them aren't even shot in nature. The praying mantis ripping off her partner's head in a moment of primal hunger or post-nut clarity may appear to be freshly fucked in a dewy forest, but in reality, she is performing in a terrarium on a sound stage. The studio doesn't want to blow their budget lying in wait in a subtropical rainforest; they hire a bug wrangler to introduce two praying mantises into a moss-filled tank. The camera starts rolling, and one mantis eats the other, or it doesn't, in which case the wrangler swaps in a mantis who understands the assignment. No one *makes* one mantis eat the other.

The production creates conditions, and then repeats those conditions until the animal acts as it should. Because really, outside the terrarium, who can say at any given moment why an animal behaves or doesn't? In the dark matter of our minds, no one can trace with perfect precision the synaptic odyssey from motivation to action. Nature's only rule is chaos.

You just want life to have meaning, which is to say, you just want him to say sorry to you. You want to correct the record. You want to correct the past, but you're in the business of space and time, and you know how that goes.

When you text Adam, you are careful not to startle him. You downplay, obscure, apologize. You pick your battles; you don't even mention that night at the bowling alley. It's a dull knife in a dense fog. You write, **there are two experiences that i really regret not bringing up sooner… i felt really manipulated… reconciling those experiences with the politics you talk about and how you've treated me in other contexts has been eating me alive every day for the past two months.**

And then you wait. You have dinner at your parents' house, sing happy birthday to your mother, push around a slice of poppyseed cake. You don't know what to expect. Probably the same limp acceptance as your many walks. He'll thank you for calling him in, he'll say sorry, it won't feel better or maybe it will.

When Adam texts you eighteen hours later, he starts with **Sorry for delay, I wanted to make sure I was alone and had time to process.** And then point by point, he categorically denies wrongdoing. **In the first scenario… You should know by now.**

You should know, but you don't. And so you try to work it out: the tectonic plates of reason butting into each other, causing disturbances. There's some slippage, some discrepancy all the more clear for how he's hidden it. He's talking to you like you asked him what happened. You hadn't asked, because you know, because you were there. He's talking to you like you're his adversary in debate club. Or like he is crafting the perfect screenshot. His language is exacting, cool to the touch. It's the language of self-preservation.

It slides into place: Adam lies.

HOW TO DO THE RIGHT THING

Much of the internet—almost the entirety of social media—is an exercise in memoir. You've learned so much about yourself from scrolling the interiority of others: the name for the shape of your eyelids, what that rash was, how to normalize the dread that coils at the base of your skull. You wrote once in your journal, which is your phone notes, the dream is getting famous for doing normal things. watching tv, getting dumped, shopping at sprouts. relatable content. relatability benefits me because it fetishizes my boringness.

The social media callout, specifically around sexual violence, is different. It's personal, but less a confessional than a witness testimony. The genre demands third-party abstraction, stripped-down language. Just the facts, ma'am. Which you understand, rationally—you are trying very hard to be rational—but this standard of clinical detachment makes the form inherently insufficient when it comes to saying things like *I said I didn't want to and then I guess I thought it was safe to leave my body or I left my body because I said I didn't want to and I saw he wasn't listening anyway and there are comets that streak through space with cores of frozen ammonia and that's kind of what happened, my body was this core of frozen poison, and I thought about this other time I normally try really hard not to think about and then he came on my dress and I washed it but I can't wear it again.*

It's funny because in many ways, the internet and the trauma brain share a language: fractured time, semiotic gaps, irregular flashes of sensory input that provoke an emotional reaction incongruent with one's present environment. In spite of this, you can't write a callout in the language of the internet. You try. You post a photo of a herd of goats swarming a tree, and the tree is labeled me and the goats are labeled boys with histories of problematic behavior who are "trying to be better" by asking me to educate and forgive them so the girls they make out with after me are fooled longer than i was. You post a screenshot of Daria from *Daria* crawling into an empty refrigerator box, and when she's in the box she says *i feel like maybe the only reason it wasn't rape is that i didn't try that hard to say no.* The internet laughs and laughs. You cannot shitpost your way through this.

Instead of the language of the internet, you must borrow from the language of law. The whole point of the callout is to supersede institutions—the cops, the courts, human resources—that overwhelmingly fail their participants. And yet, the callout replicates their litigation. This disconnect, you think, might be the basis of the callout's cringe. The smug hand-wringing, the sanctimonious self-centeredness, the way a call to action tugs at your heart: You wonder whether these vulgarities are symptoms of bridging that gap between lived truth and reportable truth. Your tools are a platform predicated on performance and a language that is historically hostile to your experience. Your task is to achieve authenticity.

You sit before a blank note in your phone. You feel like one of those fistulated cows, the ones with the plastic tube surgically implanted into their sides so liberal arts students and county fairgoers can see their guts. *Rape* feels too narrow a term; it necessitates careful documentation of exactly where the penis was in relation to the vagina, the blood alcohol levels, the precise measurement of the force of resistance. *Just the facts, ma'am.* The facts are disgusting. You want nothing to do with them, even though they have everything to do with you. In the courtroom of your mind, the prosecutor asks you if it was really so bad as all that—and if it was, why didn't you say so before? You don't want to talk about rape; the memory does not want to be put into words. It doesn't want to be put anywhere. It wants to be put down—as in, euthanized.

Sexual assault feels sterile. Like *rape*, it begs the reader to picture you naked. You imagine the internet—strangers but also your parents, also acquaintances whose altruistic distance you cherish, also people from childhood who still see you as a perfect little girl—compulsively undressing you. *Coercion. Violation.* Too euphemistic? *Abuse* defines a wide gradient of wrongdoing, from emotional manipulation to strangulation, and so its use pits your experience up against stranger danger and knife-wielding sociopaths. *It doesn't sound that bad.* You're aware of the necessity of these terms, of the privilege it requires to wield them. You're also aware that when you hit Post, Adam becomes *your abuser. My Abuser*, you picture in bubble letters on notebook paper.

You even kind of hate the phrase *I believe her. I believe her* is very different from *It happened*. It's conditional. To say *I believe* is to say *There are other possibilities, but I am making a choice*. The big joke is that if there were other possibilities, you would have chosen them. *I tried*, you want to write, but you can't.

Above all, you cannot be bitter. Which is illogical—why assume that bitterness undermines experience? The existence of pettiness does not contradict the existence of harm. It was artful of Adam to break up with you first. Now you must prove you're above saltiness. You must downplay, extenuate, acknowledge fault. Now you can't say, *the only job he's had in the past six months was assistant to a puppeteer and the puppeteer fired him. He's been lying to his family about going to work, like those family annihilators who get fired but never tell their wives and they take their briefcase and sit in the library all day, and then one day they come home and commit murder-suicide. Once he asked if he could sleep at my house because he had too many ants in his bed and I asked him how many ants was too many, and he said seven or eight, which means not only would he rather leave his house than get the ants out of his bed, but he believes six or fewer ants in the bed is reasonable*. You must be likable, sharable, marketable. Bitter, salty: words that mean *unpleasant to consume*.

The thing is, you have it as easy as anyone. He's not a millionaire, or a real celebrity, or your boss. This will be easier for you than it is for most. As a white woman, the general public has been socialized to empathize with you, to help and protect you. You have race and class and education on your side. And it is still so hard. How awful, to describe where his hands were. How cringe, to be the internet's hall monitor. How repulsive, this elective humiliation.

What's more repulsive, though, is that Adam is still posting his homemade signs. He is active in group chats. He is posting self-pitying thirst traps in his stories captioned with things like **I don't have clout. I don't have serotonin. But I do have Trader Joe.** He is sharing feminist poetry (which coincidentally is about the poet's tits). You are a rotting wooden effigy of yourself, termites boring through your brain, and he is still. So. Normal. And you are starting to think that maybe he's acting normal because for Adam, slipping off a condom or pushing a blacked-out body onto a mattress or willfully forgetting something like *I don't want to have sex tonight* isn't an anomaly. And you can't stop thinking about the walks, and Adam's insistence that he was not like other men—that he was, in fact, *better than* other men for having evolved past his base impulses in a few short weeks. His apology, how it degraded that woman, and claimed you endorsed the degradation. Adam on Tinder, using all the big words you taught him. The time you waited at a stoplight next to a high school and Adam's gaze swept across the girls in their volleyball shorts as they stretched on the blacktop and he said to you, casually, "I wonder how many of them follow me."

You are at sea on your sofa on a Saturday morning. You're waiting for a reasonable time—who posts a callout at 7:00 a.m.? Your brain is wired from insomnia, a handheld camera in your head rolling the tapes. Had it happened? Yes. Was it bad? To you, yes, and to that other girl, yes, and to future girls, maybe. Will anyone see the post? Hives bloom across your chest and crawl up your neck. With your twelve hundred followers to his sixty thousand, it feels unlikely.

One of the earliest American nature documentaries was a 1958 Disney Studios feature called *White Wilderness*. The film—described by *Variety* as "a fascinating screen experience… Filmed in awesome detail in the icy wastes of the Arctic, where struggle for existence is savage and cruel"—notably depicted what the narrator described as lemming mass suicide. Dozens of lemmings, slim and dark against the snow, dove off an icy cliff into the clean arctic air. It was a novelty of nature, the film explained, a crossed wire in the evolutionary hard drive.

Nearly three decades later, the 1982 CBC Television special *Cruel Camera* revealed that *White Wilderness* had not been shot in the Arctic. Nor were lemmings, it turned out, suicidal. The film's director had shipped a horde of lemmings to the Bow River in Alberta, Canada, purposefully disoriented them, and ran them off the cliff to their deaths. That species of lemming didn't even migrate.

It's so easy to say someone wanted it.

You press your thumb to the screen, and it's out there.

Patrick sees it first. In real life, Patrick is a father of two in some southern state and works at a program that helps children receive school lunches. On Instagram, Patrick posts 1980s fantasy art that says things like *Object permanence is a government psy-op* and *I hope they serve looks in hell*. Patrick sees the callout in your stories, screenshots and reposts them. Then Allie reposts them. Then Margot, then Axel and Helen and Shelly. Refresh, refresh, refresh. You sit on the floor by the toilet and tug the screen with your thumb.

Your phone vibrates like it's being electrically shocked. It kind of is, you think, and so are you, buzzing with the force of your own actions. You watch your story spin out into the void of Instagram until you can't see it anymore, and your phone still vibrates.

You get many, many messages. They are overwhelmingly, shockingly kind. Black hearts drift from one corner of the universe to yours, rain down on your face from your phone screen. There are detractors, of course. The normal misogynistic ones, and the guy who wants to piss on you, and the woman who finds your personal email address and sends you a 2,364-word treatise on how your anger benefits no one. She asks if you are, perhaps, *missing the perspective of the abuser*. She uses your first name a lot when she writes, as if she is reaching through the screen to cup your chin in her hand and gently shake it. You track her IP address to a mid-size city in Texas and pull your mouse across Google Maps. And then you get a message that reads

> Hi. Adam sent me a nonconsensual video of him masturbating last year. We had dm'd a few times but it wasn't like that, I did not want it and it made me uncomfortable. Sorry you went thru it too

Radio waves breaching the atmosphere. A message from a foreign planet. Your phone shudders. In your phone, another woman is making contact. And another. Messages and emails. You hold the phone three inches from your face and waves of blue light crash over you, one after another after another.

> I have never met a man who tried so hard to get me to change my mind after I said no. I have never had to defend myself against a man like that.

> I was an assistant and he was this cool older employee so I tried to ignore the weird vibes...He grabbed my hips and I told him I wanted to leave and he pushed me down and said I had to kiss him first.

> I told him I didn't wanna have sex but then he grabbed me and wouldn't stop and I felt so uncomfortable, I just went numb.

* * *

> The same thing happened to me last summer.
> We had sex when I didn't want to. I had a lot of
> complicated feelings about it, mostly denial…
> but I want you to know I'm sorry I didn't say or
> do anything that might have stopped this from
> happening to you.
>
> I'm crying and shaking. What you went through
> sounds exactly like my experience with Adam.
> Part of me has wondered for years when this
> would happen, but also I really really hoped I was
> the last.

You're vaguely aware that you're hyperventilating. Letters blur and rearrange themselves. Faces are attached to profiles. Some are young—really young—and some are your age. Overwhelmingly, you get the sense that you've seen them before. You've browsed the same stacks at the bookstore on Sunset, paddled swan boats past one another on Echo Park Lake. Two of them, you later learn, found you because they're friends with two of your more amicable exes. Adam found them because they were a classmate, a fan, a fellow comedian, an employee, a friend.

You read and read and read. I'm sorry, you write. I'm so sorry. It's supposed to feel validating. Comforting, to know it wasn't just you. Instead, you feel overfed: a foie gras goose, gullet wrenched open, forcibly pumped with the sadness of others. Our Idiot Goose of Sorrow. Just one of so many.

There's also, in your inbox, another screenshot. This one, shared quietly by an online mutual, isn't a confession or an accusation. It's an internal email from the media startup. Alongside a screenshot of the Facebook post, the email contains instructions from some higher-up to remove Adam from socials and take him off the freelancer index. Also, to contact him about the incident.

The time stamp on the email is from June. You texted Adam the same screenshot in August, in what would have in any other time in history been butterfly season. **Woah this is really upsetting,** he'd texted back. He'd already known about it for months.

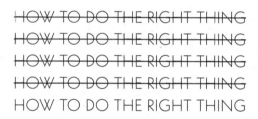

The hillside streets of Silver Lake are narrow, winding, and nearly bereft of streetlights. You could park a few streets down and wear dark clothing. The trick would be not to freeze. You are disgustingly prone to freezing. But if you caught him off-guard—if you caught him off-guard, there wouldn't be time. You could use anything. A rope around the neck: his face red, gray, slack. A cigarette and a rag soaked in turpentine. In your head, though, it's a crowbar. More length, maybe—more distance. The kind of thing that, when cutting through the air, sounds like a bird alighting from a telephone wire. You imagine him turning toward you as the crowbar falls through space, submitting to the law of gravity. Once, when he was feeling depressed, he'd texted you asking you to cheer him up, and you'd recycled an old group therapy exercise and asked him to tell you something he was proud of. My hairline, he'd answered. The crack would sound like a watermelon hitting the ground, you think. Sharp and wet. They wouldn't hear it from the big house. It'd take less than ten minutes. And then you could take Trader Joe up in your arms and slip out the side door. You can almost feel the cool air, Trader Joe's warm weight. This could be the start of something new for both of you.

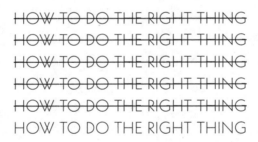

HOW TO DO THE RIGHT THING

Whereas the function of most posts is to connect—whether through the bindings of relatability or aspiration—the callout post's function is alienation. It's the othering of the person being called out, sure, but also the writer; to draft a callout is to enter into the assumption that the reader is on the other side of a rhetorical chasm. You must build a bridge of language to reach them. You must work to be believed.

You have never felt more witnessed or more lonely. You are floating above the earth, watching life unfold without you. This otherness physically hurts: heartburn, nausea, a flu-like dissociative ache that moves between your brain and body the way a ghost drifts through its haunted house. You quit drinking. You've always been toxically jealous of people who claim to eat less when they're stressed, but you're sleeping through meals. You go to a party and eat a stranger's MDMA and feel normal for three hours and doubly crummy for three days. You go to the park with a friend and her friend turns to you coolly and says, "My friend knows Adam, and she thinks you made it up. By the way."

Sometimes you feel bubble wrapped, the world blurry and untouchable. Sometimes you're coiled like a spring, entirely present—the animalistic presence of fear. *Fight, flight, freeze, appease.* Your hands shake. Stupid. Who could you attack with shaking hands?

You can't stop thinking about the other women. You study their avatars, their tiny circle-cropped faces. They're pretty. An evil thought punctures your sadness, or maybe bolsters it, a pole for this circus: *Prettier than me.* Each of their stories compounds your own shame. Why couldn't you leave like they could? They share their encounters in horror, in solidarity, and they ask you not to share them publicly. It's fair—it's what you would want, probably, if you hadn't been you—but you feel like a cracked vessel leaking anger. In the court of public opinion, you are a lone hysteric. Privately, you're the project manager of a shared trauma endeavor. You're angry at them, which feels most shameful of all. *Survivors.*

Sisters in healing. Draw a line between any haphazard cluster of stars, and you'll have a constellation.

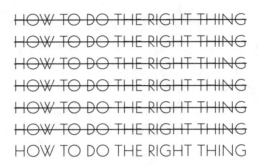

The accused's rebuttal, for all the fanfare and fearmongering around digital pile-ons, tends to be relatively low lift. It only has to offer enough deniability that the reader can justify their natural resistance to expending the energy it takes to change one's mind. *Don't lather yourself up over nothing*, it soothes.

You don't hear about Adam's public apology until it's nearly expired from his Instagram stories. Which makes sense, maybe, since he isn't speaking to you. He speaks about you: a *recent ex* who believes he may have *misread some signs*. He forwent the notes app, instead opting for a bright blue colorway that better matches his brand. He refers to himself as—potentially, so he's heard, because he is listening—*pushy*. He isn't a predator; he's a victim of toxic masculinity. This has been a major learning experience for him. And anyway, he emphasizes, he had just broken up with the accuser, so, make of that what you will.

He never mentions the other women. He mentions strange details, like claiming you'd watched a movie before he raped you, when you have no memory of a movie. Was he lying? Or maybe he was mistaken, because he couldn't remember what day it was that the rape had occurred, because they all blended together. It's possible, you realize, that he's thinking of someone else. The whole thing evokes, for you, a lab grown thing trying to bleed. A high-tech vegan meat patty. Adam ends it by apologizing to his fans. He is sorry, he says, for letting down his audience.

You hold the private trauma and the public belittlement. You scroll back in your phone and realize that one woman's experience with him occurred *one day* after your first call-in walk. You contain yourself.

Days later, Adam texts you privately—

> **ADAM:** I'm sorry for removing my condom during sex without ensuring you were aware. This is assault. I'm sorry for pursuing sex on a night on which you'd made it clear you weren't interested. On these occasions I violated your consent, trust, safety and basic dignity; I abused you emotionally and physically.

—which is insane, considering that he already publicly declared you a liar. To admit this to you now feels like a cruel inside joke. You're shaken by the contact, but more so by his ability to move through the world with each foot in a separate reality, his pathological refusal to acknowledge where the two dimensions must merge. You don't know where your feet are. How strange that you had spent so much time thinking you were the withholding one, when really, you didn't know him at all.

~~HOW TO DO THE RIGHT THING~~
~~HOW TO DO THE RIGHT THING~~
~~HOW TO DO THE RIGHT THING~~
~~HOW TO DO THE RIGHT THING~~
~~HOW TO DO THE RIGHT THING~~
~~HOW TO DO THE RIGHT THING~~
~~HOW TO DO THE RIGHT THING~~
HOW TO DO THE RIGHT THING

When you quit, you tell production that you're leaving to pursue your dreams. An executive producer corners you in the bullpen. You're lazy, he reminds you. You're giving up on the only good thing you have going for you. He asks gleefully, "How are you going to survive?"

You go to somatic experience therapy and punch a pillow in slow motion. You go to group therapy and write your name on a binder in pink marker and fill the binder with violent evil thoughts. You go to Planned Parenthood for an STD panel. You go to your art school friend's amateur group therapy party. You gaze into a stranger's eyes and mirror their body language, lifting the corners of your lips with theirs. After mirroring, there's a sort of sharing circle. You're seated across from an elfin terror in a doll-sized cashmere sweater with whom at least three group members are in love, your art school friend told you beforehand, your friend included. You feel the heat of the terror's eyes on you while you share, because the whole point is sharing, and this is you now. Your whole personality is fear and anger. You have no creative projects, no romantic foibles, no curiosity. You miss denial, you tell the group. And her eyes narrow. You know that tilt of the chin: Your pain is *boring*. You are another girl with a *trauma share*, a mess of weakness and self-centeredness and a childish insistence that the world should be fair.

You drink tea and mingle and wish that you could just be normal. The terror keeps her distance, but another girl approaches you, dark-haired and soft-spoken. You think it must be because she feels sorry for you.

"I messaged you," she says.

~~HOW TO DO THE RIGHT THING~~
~~HOW TO DO THE RIGHT THING~~
~~HOW TO DO THE RIGHT THING~~
~~HOW TO DO THE RIGHT THING~~
~~HOW TO DO THE RIGHT THING~~
~~HOW TO DO THE RIGHT THING~~
~~HOW TO DO THE RIGHT THING~~

YOU HAVE A NEW MEMORY

~~HOW TO DO THE RIGHT THING~~
HOW TO DO THE RIGHT THING

The bowling alley advertised free parking, but when you arrive you discover the underground lot is hardly more than a series of coffin-sized slots girded by door-scraping beams. It reeks of piss and petrichor. You're a phenomenal parallel parker; you parallel park like it's a party trick, like you're tying a cherry stem into a knot with your tongue. You've worked parallel parking into every dating profile you've ever written. Head-in, somehow, is nearly impossible. In the parking lot of the bowling alley, you pause. This bowling alley is different: It's miles away, in a busy strip of K-Town, and the lanes are new and no one covers Jimmy Buffett. There's a vending machine that dispenses cotton ankle socks pricked with tiny hearts.

The girl who posted on Facebook is named Kayla. She's a Florida transplant with gray-green eyes that sparkle when she's stoned, which is always. When she first reached out over DM, you'd exchanged a few high-strung messages about sisterhood and then studiously avoided her. At first it was awful, that collision with the dark-haired girl—Olivia, who until then had only been a story like yours—at the art school party. You were knocked off balance, out of orbit. You had spent so much time in Adam's presence, moving your body around his body. And here was another body. Another way. Her realness took your breath away.

After Olivia, you apologized to Kayla, for everything, and Kayla invited you to join her bowling league. This is how you meet in real life: You are frozen in the parking lot, and she is balancing a vape pen between her lips and waving you into a spot with a slightly impatient assertiveness you find comforting.

In a few weeks, international news sources will report that the host of the nature show attempted to assault his assistant, then professionally punished her after she evaded his advances. Two additional women will come forward. One will comment that the host had groped her under the guise of looking at a tattoo. The show will be released a year behind schedule, to critical acclaim.

Adam will refrain from posting on Instagram for three weeks, and then he will rebrand himself as a survivor of cancel culture. His audience will quickly surpass a hundred thousand followers. Later, under an infographic posted by an anti-cancel-culture influencer, he will comment, I've lived through over 2 years of stalking, harassment, misrepresentation, demonization—you haven't spoken to him since his deranged apology, will never, you hope, speak to him again—the fact that I still believe in myself, my dreams and the inherent goodness at the core of all people gives me a pride no one can take from me. You'll read this, and you'll picture Adam's hand on his dick, his face red. In his eyes, the reflection of a woman's expression as it shifts, water-like, from confusion to fear. *I thought I said no.* In his mind's eye, himself. His goodness.

When the other girls in the bowling league ask how you and Kayla met, you make silent sideways eye contact. "Internet," Kayla says.

You toss ball after ball into the gutter. You eat chicken tenders and only briefly do your thoughts linger on the sanitary implications of shoving your fingers into the communal holes of the bowling ball, and then using those same fingers to ferry a snack into your mouth. Occasionally you gaze down the long, dark lanes while everyone laughs around you. Once, when you're pulled into the black hole of the pin drop, Kayla lightly shoves your knee as if to say, *Where'd you go?* You come back.

You come back week after week. You buy yourself bowling shoes and a child-sized ball with butterflies on it. Because the thing about bowling is, it's about the wrist. No one in the bowling alley can say, with certainty, how the tilt of the lane and the polish on the ball and the rotting foundation of the building and how much protein you ate that day might change your game. No one knows how the present affects the future. The ball in midair, the arc of it, the collision: It's a miracle, if you think about it.

You stand at the top of the lane. You plant your feet and look ahead. You do what you can. You twist your wrist slightly—so slightly—in the wild hope that somewhere else—distanced by time, space, gravity—you'll make an impact.

IN REAL LIFE

MY FAITH FIRST wavers in the train station parking lot. It's not really even a station—there's no ticket booth or shaded bench, just a scythe of pavement cleaving the railroad tracks, a half-flight of concrete steps, and a gravel dugout. The train from Paris was an inrush of rolling farmland and blazing expanses of mustard and the dancing specular light of phone screens on the train car's ceiling. The connecting station had a ticket machine, an espresso machine, and a vending machine that dispensed wedges of fresh Comté. Winding farther into the countryside, every house had a trampoline in the yard. All this bucolic wonder and you could still be bored. As we pulled into the village, I saw a pair of listless children sitting on the sun-drenched mesh of one, inhaling the scent of warm plastic.

I look for habits. Would they wear habits? Lots of nuns, I read on the internet, have updated their wardrobes to include cotton skirts and tasteful khaki chore coats. A few even wear denim, to better identify with the common man. They're invested in volunteering and protesting and cave-aging small-batch cheddar. I chose Benedictines because the order has a tradition of hospitality, and because the names of the abbeys are beautiful: Saint Mary-of-the-Woods. Sisters of Perpetual Adoration. Our Lady of Grace.

I chose this abbey over the others for its renunciation of aesthetic indulgence, which is to say, its web design. The few photographs available online are dimly lit and strangely cropped: a wooden chair positioned ominously in the corner of an otherwise empty room; a close-up shot of part of an unidentified painted landscape, taken with the flash on. On another abbey's website, the nuns had a Monastic Live Webcam that streamed prayer services the way some national parks stream salmon. The webcam was positioned in a high corner of the chapel, like a security camera. The space was airy and modern: light wood, clear glass, a whiff of celebrity megachurch. Half a dozen women in gabardine robes sat in stackable chairs in silence. I watched them pray and I felt like a pervert.

I'd unadvisedly packed a pair of Los Angeles Apparel long-sleeve cotton shirts without trying them on; the one I'm wearing is child-sized, stifling and slutty all at the same time. I button my jacket over my stomach and wonder if my jacket is starting to smell. A car pulls into the dugout and idles, and my heart leaps, and then the only other person in the parking lot—a middle-aged woman with a duffel bag, whom I'd hubristically clocked as a potential abbess—approaches the window, waving. It's six o'clock on a Tuesday in the kind of town where everyone goes home for a nap at three. The car pulls away. This station, this corner, this village: empty. I don't have the abbey's phone number; it occurs to me that they might not have a phone at all. And anyway, somewhere along the Swiss border I'd lost reception, my browser apologetically gray, the pulsing dot of my location gone still. The green dot: my existence concentrated to a fine point. I have, without noticing, disappeared. But isn't doubt just the maligned cousin of possibility? I flip through error screens on my useless phone, then turn it off.

A silver van swerves into the parking lot with such vigor that it nearly taps my luggage. A man unfolds himself from the front seat, emerging in pieces: ginger beard, plaid button-down, slim gray canvas pants, high-top sneakers. No priest's collar. He has ingenue eyes, blue and perpetually widened in wonder or confusion. When he confirms I'm there for the monastery as if I'm not the only person in the parking lot, his grin reveals quaintly crooked teeth.

John, I learn on the half-hour drive past sparkling streams and fields of the sort of cows that model for organic milk cartons, is some sort of cloistral assistant. He's affable, delighted by my delight at the sight of livestock. His English is better than my French, but small talk is still an amicable struggle. I took French all through high school but my teacher was from Poughkeepsie and so my accent is bizarre and embarrassing, and I'm too self-conscious about it to speak anything beyond a few well-worn sentences.

John manages the abbey with his wife, Fabienne. He smells like something I can't place, woody and sweet, faintly animal. As we drive the forest closes around us like we're telling a gossipy story. The road becomes a dirt path flanked by a stone wall, and then there's the abbey. It's less a building than a complex: a thousand years of haphazard renovations, an expansive mélange of marble, stone, wood, and plaster in shades of mottled pink and gray. It appears to have been built into the hillside, one side butting up against the forest. Trees swell above us. I look up and have the sudden image of a wave poised to crash. At its crest, a glinting metal cross pokes through the pines.

My parents, like so many of their generation, were raised Catholic in the wooden paddle days and later sought ablution in acid-laced lemonade and Jerry Garcia's sweat. Agnostics themselves, they enrolled my siblings and me in Catholic school as a sort of reverse psychology experiment: They feared that if they raised us godless, we would fill that spiritual deficit with fanaticism and they'd have to deal with insufferable dogmatism at faraway Christmas dinners. Better to disillusion us early. At home we were casually Catholic: I was allowed to watch *Beavis and Butt-Head* and take the Lord's name in vain, but I couldn't pet a stranger's dog without my mom comparing me to Saint Francis. I was a solitary and fearful kid, haunted by a nonspecific shame. I liked the small pencils the church stashed between the pews for signing alms checks.

My strongest memory of Catholic school is sitting at the back of the first-grade classroom, one small hand in the air, besieged by a powerful need to shit. Mrs. Mortar had a dome of box-dyed hair and a wardrobe of desaturated floral prints that decades later might be characterized as *coastal grandma*. She taught us that while most crucifixion art depicts stigmata in the palms, the nails were actually driven through the soft tissue of the wrists, between the radius and ulna bones, to hold the body aloft and prolong suffering. She only let one child go to the bathroom at a time. I remember my classmates trotting obediently out the classroom door as my gut churned. I caught Mrs. Mortar's eye and waved my arm frantically, mouthed *Emergency*. Mrs. Mortar held my gaze, reminded the class that well-behaved children go first, and called on someone else. The meek shall inherit the earth. I shit my shorts.

I sat quietly in my own waste for the rest of the day, endured whispers of disgust, tried not to move my legs too much as I shuffled to the car in my soiled khakis. In the container of my mom's Volvo, the smell was unbearable. The ruse was up, my mom forced to pull over and peel my tights off in a McDonald's bathroom stall, swearing bombastically. That was the first time someone I loved asked what was wrong with me. I couldn't understand her frustration. I had followed directions. In my memory the tights she shoved into the sanitary bin were my favorite, snowy white and speckled with cartoon dalmatian puppies, but I don't think the school dress code would have allowed that. That's devotion: a candle for the parts that don't make sense. I recently tried to find the same tights online, but nothing came up except polyester dog costumes on happy children who never shit their pants. During the search, my phone kept autocorrecting *dalmatian* to *salvation*.

* * *

John insists on lugging my suitcase into the courtyard, a garden of slender willows and neatly trimmed hedges circling a murky fountain. The grounds are still and I wonder whether the nuns are in mass, if I'm disrupting a sacred moment. I recall some online image of a trail of cloaked devotees trudging up a hill at dusk, heads bowed in reverence. I follow John and imagine myself atop a mountain, prostrate before the setting sun.

Off the courtyard there's a welcome center with postcards and miniature wooden crucifixes for sale and, beyond that, a small table where John hands me a disconcerting number of liability waivers.

"Can you read that?" he asks, and I honestly tell him I can't, and he shrugs. "Bureaucracy. The French love it." I sign them all. The last sheet, he tells me, pledges my allegiance to the Carthusian brotherhood.

"The brotherhood," I say.

"Yes, yes—though they can't be here." John doesn't elucidate whether this is for religious or scheduling reasons. He glances at and then files away the documents that allow me to die here without consequence.

"And...the nuns?"

John's eyes widen to full aperture. "Nuns?"

What clueless, cruel Mrs. Mortar once marked down as *a lack of curiosity* and *easily succumbs to peer pressure* I might reframe as a willingness to open oneself to the world: a tender receptivity. When I learn that there is no community of nuns, justice-loving or otherwise, at my Benedictine retreat, and that in fact it's not at all a Benedictine convent but a Carthusian cloister, in which one spends fourteen hours a day in a stone cell, silent but for the three to four hours of mandatory prayer, I surrender. I have the next ten days, after all, to contemplate fate, and whether I saw nuns on the website, or whether, in a fit of late-night mistranslation, I may have emailed the wrong monastery.

Sequestration is often imposed when one is deemed very good or very bad. The effects of isolation in prisoners are well documented: loss of concentration, loss of memory, obsessive and violent thought patterns, paranoia, suicidal ideation, hallucinations, psychosis. The UN categorizes solitary confinement for more than fifteen days as a form of torture.

Self-imposed solitude, on the other hand, is a fundamental sacred experience. Reclusion is a pre-Christian, nearly global spiritual practice; while its exact origins are untraceable, anthropological evidence suggests eremitism has existed as long as humans have had social groups from which to escape.

It takes some effort to disentangle what I know of cloistered women from what I think I know of cloistered women, which is tinged with group singalongs and lesbianism and the occasional bout of Satanism. Considered a sort of living sacrifice to the church, medieval women were confined to abbeys not unlike the one I expected to join, or isolated more drastically: In the initiation ritual of the anchoress, her cell was dug out into a grave. Accompanied by a choir's funeral dirges, the devoted processed from the church to the cell and crawled into her burial pit. Before locking her in the enclosure, the celebrant sprinkled over her a fistful of dirt.

Spiritual sequestration is meant to punish—as the ascetic monk Dorotheus of Thebes succinctly wrote of his body, "It kills me, so I kill it"—but it's also a means to an end: mortification of the flesh, the deadening of human sensation to heighten awareness of the holy. There is a fascinating tension between the derealization of the body and the creation of art. In the liminal state of quarantine, the twelfth-century nun Hildegard of Bingen was struck by debilitatingly painful tongues of flame that carried angelic harmonies. From her trances she manifested surreal illuminated manuscripts and strange, florid music; she is widely regarded today as one of the world's earliest and most innovative composers. In her own solitude, the anchoress Julian of Norwich encountered the Virgin Mary as a little girl and Jesus as a rotting corpse. She recounted these visions over the late fourteenth and early fifteenth centuries in *Revelations of Divine Love*, the earliest confirmed work written by a woman in the English language. I wanted to abscond to a nunnery because I was captivated by Hildegard and Julian and the quixotic weirdness of their art, and also because only an extreme experience of compulsory deprivation might return the nameless thing I've lost.

The problem came on slowly, like delayed-onset tinnitus: one day I notice the whole world's pitch is off, and in the moment of noticing I realize it's been like that for a long time. Every opinion I have is someone else's, baby bird food I suck down and turn around and spit into someone else's throat. Every fact is flanked by a targeted ad. A scaly rash has bloomed around my eyelids. At night I check the doors and the windows and the burners on the stove, and then I check each of my accounts, one by one, to make sure I didn't post anything stupid, and then I check them again. I can't sleep through the night and I can't endure the day without retreating to my bed to rot: Ophelia in a pool of blue light. A ringing in the ears.

While disappointingly vacant of nuns, the Carthusian cloisters operate under a similar pretense of mysticism. Per my rudimentary understanding of the cloister's welcome packet, Saint Bruno of Cologne established the first Carthusian monastery with the support of a bishop who'd received a prophetic image of the monk resplendent under a garland of stars. I feel relatively apathetic toward the hollow-eyed TikTok TradCaths and their persnickety rules—my culture, your costume, et cetera—but I am awed, sometimes, by closed circuits of devotion, what it means to follow and have followers at all. The twentieth-century mystic Simone Weil wrote, "Attention is the rarest and purest form of generosity." I want so badly to believe that at the core of me is something bloody and beating and true, and if I could shut the fuck up, like a shy animal it would reveal itself to me. My life feels like it's out the train window, a blur of motion and consequence, the seat facing backward so I charge blindly into the future. I want divine reorientation. I want to suck sugar from the palm of God's hand.

★ ★ ★

The first rule of the cloisters is to honor your vow of silence. The second is to write John a note if your silence induces a mental breakdown. I will not spend two weeks with my sisters in Christ, but on Sunday a priest will come to give me *le pardon de Dieu*—God's forgiveness. Apparently structured to maximize monotony, the day is divided by prayers: lauds at 8:00 a.m., vespers at 4:15 p.m., and compline at 9:00 p.m. Lunch is at noon and dinner at seven. Breakfast is any time before lauds and consists of a self-serve station in the kitchen, bowls of fruit and plastic-wrapped *biscotte* toasts and tea and instant coffee. I ask John if we're allowed to take snacks from the bowls between meals, and the question seems to upset him. He purses his lips in contemplation, then concedes that I can take toasts to my room at night, as long as I eat them in the morning.

If you removed the plaster Virgin Mary, the kitchen is unremarkable, even corporate: a sink, a fridge, a microwave, a metal table, a whiteboard, a shelf of wooden crates. When John and I tour it, someone has set the table with three salad plates and three glass tureens of soup. On the whiteboard is a menu and a lettered grid. I've been assigned cell E, John says, and so to indicate that I've received dinner I must mark the space under E with a cross. I'm not sure whether he means an X or a Christian cross. There's only one other mark on the board, under B, and B has either unintentionally drawn an X with a flourish that connects the upper and lower left points, or intentionally drawn a rudimentary ichthys, also known as a Jesus fish. John hands me a dry erase marker. I draw a Jesus fish too. John says nothing that might indicate whether this is the correct choice. Instead, he directs me to a wooden crate with the letter E marked on the lid and a dowel handle affixed to the top that makes me think of a cardboard cat carrier. The front panel of each box slides up to reveal two compartments, inside which are a set of silverware, a water glass, a small carafe, a ceramic cup, and a cloth napkin.

We take my crate of soup out of the kitchen and across the courtyard, through a set of imposing wooden doors and into a dark corridor thick with the primitive stench of moss. My suitcase slaps grotesquely against the uneven floors. And then we cross another threshold, and the hall is bathed in aquatic evening light: the inner wall has opened into a row of ceiling-high arched windows, panes sugary with age, that snake around an atrium of trembling apple trees.

John stops at a door marked with a scribble of Latin and, beneath the inscription, the letter E. He procures a heavy iron key. He demonstrates unlocking the door, which I find patronizing until I realize it's a precise choreography: insert the key all the way into the lock until it passes clean through the door into the darkness beyond; pull it back slowly, halfway; make a soft scooping motion with your wrist as you turn it. I jiggle the lock futilely.

"Go slowly," John says. "You have the time."

After much embarrassment, the door to cell E jerks open into a narrow landing, the divider between upper and lower levels. Downstairs, what to the novice might appear to be an instrument of torture—a table with metal spikes and cranks and vises—is in fact a wood borer, John explains, with which monks once crafted the boxes in which Chartreuse liqueur is sold. From the craft corner, we step into a misshapen square of bricks and weeds, insulated by a high stone wall: my private garden.

Upstairs, a lachrymose plaster bust of Christ dominates the landing, head tilted so as to contemplate the floor. Through another door, what John calls the Ave Maria room: large and drafty, empty except for an armoire, three boxes of twigs and newspapers, and, on the boarded-up fireplace mantel, a wooden Madonna the size and shape of a bowling pin. "So when you walk in, you can pray to her," John says. I thank him like I've had trouble in the past walking into a room and knowing to whom I should pray.

Finally, through the Ave Maria room: my bedroom. It's less ascetic than expected. There's a slender bed with a deflated-looking mattress, a bay window with a table fitted into the nook, a desk with a red ink blotter and a heavy blond wood Bible stand, and a woodstove. The hallway to the bathroom has been converted into a prayer portal, with a little bench for kneeling and a terra-cotta crucifix. John asks if I know how to operate a woodstove, and I say yes, even though I don't. John asks if I need anything else, and I say no, even though I'm not sure. John leaves, and I'm alone.

The soup, now cold, is carrot, served with vinegar-laced greens. I try to consume it in small, mindful spoonfuls as I look out the window. The sky is the color of a nickel. There's the garden wall; an expanse of grass, trimmed with another stone wall; a field of grazing horses; a forested hillside; and through the trees, a slice of road.

I'm always looking for an emergency exit. It's the kind of neurosis based in just enough reason that you keep indulging it: compulsive preparedness for fires and earthquakes and murderers, some mix of gender conditioning and egocentricity. I suck soup between my teeth. I think about all the doors we passed to get here, all the walls, each of them solid stone two feet thick. The two-story drop from the bay window to the garden would be painful, but maybe survivable, if I hit dirt. Once there, though, my options narrow. The garden walls are too high and mossy to scale, even if I use the Virgin Mary prayer enclave as a foothold. My cell is separated from the rest of the monastery by an iron lock and a maze of stone chambers, and the rest of the monastery is separated from the world by untold miles of wilderness. I lay down my spoon and listen. Nothing but the echo of metal on glass.

A notice tacked above the woodstove draws attention to arson and carbon monoxide poisoning. Keep the windows open, add the last log before compline. I stick my head as far out the window as it'll go. The garden wall slopes so that my cell is cut off from whatever lies on either side of it. If I set the room ablaze, or have a stroke, or am attacked by entities earthly or demonic, no one will come for me.

Back in the kitchen, the dishwashing sponge is limp and filthy. It has the texture of bread that has been soaked in milk, the green side smoothed to a felted matte from months of food waste frottage. The kitchen isn't properly ventilated and so the sponge never dries, and bacteria swarm across it in rapturous orgies and then crawl onto my silverware. We return our clean dishes to the table, but the silverware and glassware we keep in our box; I picture my water glass sweating in its cubby, cloudy with germs.

A man enters the kitchen: a blur of dark clothing as I avert my eyes. We're not supposed to interact, but I don't know to what extent we're meant to ignore each other. I face the sink and twist the tap so the water is scalding and wash my dishes quickly. When I pass him on my way out, the man has turned to the wall and stands perfectly still, like a Sim.

My first *office*—like mass, but somehow not—is compline, and when I arrive the chapel is dark. I bought a cheap analog wristwatch for this experience but couldn't find a clock with which to sync it, so I wound it back ten minutes just in case. I dawdle outside the door by a table of dog-eared psalm books and laminated packets of prayers marked with sticky tabs. Across the hall, a second table holds cubbies and slips of paper for note writing. I wonder if anyone has ever abused the system—you could have a whole silent affair via erotic letters, if you wanted. Under the cubbies is a pile of incomprehensible maps. There's the monastery in a nest of dotted and solid lines, and some cryptic slashes of pink highlighter. There's the cross on the mountain, floating off to the left. When my watch reads twelve past, I make a move.

The chapel's interior is a high school art history test: a squinched dome above the altar, a choir, a nave. You don't sit in a pew, like in normal church; instead, the sides of the choir are lined with aisles, and the aisles have individual stations: fold-down seats separated by panels of thick dark wood, like they don't want you to cheat off your neighbor. I choose a station and sit very still. The altar is all candles and Easter lilies under a colossal crucifix. Despite its heft, there's something delicate about the carving—some suggestion of motion. One of Christ's hands is nailed to the cross, but the other reaches out to brush the air.

Bodies trail in. I pretend to study my prayer packet. Strange, to assemble like this, in silence, in the dark. It feels very clandestine, which makes it feel very official. Everyone else bows to the crucifix before taking their seat, except a man who is maybe the man from the kitchen, who falls to his knees and touches his forehead to the floor. I pick out John, who unwraps a thick length of rope from the wall and tugs until a bell peals somewhere far above us. Fabienne, I gather, is the flickering slice of profile lighting candles. When our small circle is lambent, she settles besides John, and then she begins to sing. The word she sings is *Hallelujah*, silent H, four syllables stretched into a meandering path of a prayer.

There is a lot of sitting and standing and bowing. There are parts one sings, and parts one listens to, and intervals of silence. I can't get a foothold on the melody, the pauses and pick-ups and held notes. Psalms are a somber affair, less sung than lamented. Ecclesiastical French is filled with words I wouldn't know in English. John intermittently barks a number and I frantically flip through my psalm book, getting it right half the time. We sing *Hallelujah* again, and then Fabienne snuffs the candles and John leaves, and we trail out behind him. Everyone bows to Christ again, and so I do, too.

YOU HAVE A NEW MEMORY

* * *

I wash my face for sixty seconds, like I read on Reddit. I push my moisturizer into my skin, rather than smear it—rolling my hands, reddening my cheeks—because a beautiful woman on TikTok showed me how. I let each layer of product dry for five to seven minutes before applying the next. I sit on the toilet and my hands feel empty and my life feels empty. I can't google *ivermectin azelaic acid correct order*. I can't google *how to pray with rosary*.

In the Ave Maria room, I whisper a Hail Mary and then I check the furniture to make sure no one is hiding in it. I shut the door of my bedroom and block it with my suitcase.

I wake clammy, panicked, reaching for something. Around me the dark expands like the eyes of a slug.

My anxieties are base and human, the sort of worries Jesus promises to fix on billboards along desert highways. Various people are various levels of mad at me. I inadvertently posted my breasts on the internet before turning off my phone. I didn't pay my last dermatology copay, and when I get back my credit will be tanked. When I get back, I will be hacked. When I get back, I will be canceled. There are abandoned mines outside Vegas that are so deep that if you throw in a quarter, you'll never hear it hit the bottom. There is someone in the history of time who has thrown a live animal into those mines. Several, probably. In my head, in the dark, a parade of doomed adorable creatures I'm powerless to save. I think if you jump off a building or bridge and it's high enough, the air knocks you unconscious or maybe even kills you outright before you hit the ground. But still—before that—that fear. To suffer and not know why: the burden of limited consciousness. Blooms of dirty-sponge-induced bacteria overtake my coffee cup. My worst college ex-boyfriend will join the Italian American heritage social club and I won't be able to go to the monthly pasta platter anymore.

In the face of anxiety, therapists will tell you to check the facts. The problem is, the facts are in my phone. Monasteries were early centers of Scholasticism; there's no evidence to suggest that monks wouldn't love the internet, that quiet, concentrated place to increase knowledge, to seek answers. If we are soft mysteries of flesh and voltage, pressing ourselves against the world to understand it, is it not sacred to access a cloud of information? It's Wednesday morning, which means it's Tuesday night in California, which means the Italian American heritage social club just held their membership meeting and have posted the new recruits in their Instagram stories. If I looked from my burner account, it would be like I was never even there.

When the sky lightens to a marbled blue I walk to the kitchen for a sachet of crystallized coffee and two packets of *biscotte* toast. Crystallized coffee tastes like an espresso fart with a gasoline finish. To minimize wear on my dinner napkin, I delegate a crumb napkin from the two extras I packed in my suitcase. For the nuns, I packed cloth napkins, bed linens, an assortment of modest long-sleeve tees and turtlenecks, two pairs of pants, two long skirts, the only bra I own that isn't lingerie, an embarrassment of underwear, a freezer bag of skincare products, an alarm clock, my watch, and my first communion rosary. The rosary is made of tin and pearlescent plastic beads. I packed a knuckle-sized hunk of smoky quartz and a dozen types of medications and vitamins in a rainbow plastic days-of-the-week case. I packed nail polish, deludedly, because I thought maybe I could paint the nuns' nails, and they would see my heart is pure.

I eat my brittle toast hunched over the crumb napkin and then, to clean it, I wave it out the window like a pale flag.

John yanks the chapel bell several times before it starts ringing, which is maybe how all bells work. I count the peals but find no pattern; the clangs don't correlate to time, and every *office* the number changes. He loosens his grip and lets the rope run through his fist.

John raps the wood of his seat three times and we stand and he says a little something in French. We chant *Hallelujah* six times in various keys. Fabienne calls to us, and we respond. I hold my rosary limply in one hand.

In periods of reverent silence, I take in the others. To my left sits John, then Fabienne, who is slight and sensible-looking. To my right, just visible past my partition, there's a woman with silver cumulous hair wearing a plastic slicker. Across from me sits an elderly man who leans on a cane and chants gutturally, and next to him is the man from the kitchen, who fascinates me. It's impossible to know how old he is in the stormy morning half-light, but with his skinny jeans and square glasses and zip-up hoodie, he looks like he'd write for a music magazine in 2009. I try to imagine him engaged in Vatican II discourse with a Kierkegaard reading, eating disordered godpilled e-girl. He bobs and sways to the psalms like they're songs with melodies and not atonal dirges, his eyes closed, his fingers laced delicately. Sometimes he drops his head into his hands.

The cloisters are an architectural enigma: spirals and dead ends, sudden precarious staircases, passages that twist into darkness. The atrium across from my front door turns out to be a cemetery. I tell myself, at four in the morning, that the monks are in heaven and therefore too busy to haunt me. Doors beget more doors, and all the doors stick so you can't tell what's locked and what's stuck, and so it feels like you're trying to break into everywhere. Which I am, I guess. I'm searching for a new sponge.

First, I find the wood room: metal pens of tinder and tree stumps studded with glinty hatchets. I find a barred metal door, like in a prison, and through the grate nothing but feathery black. I find, in a hallway, a basin of water designed to look like a grotto with stucco stalactites and in the center, a sinister Madonna and child. Her expression invokes a memory of calling to a kitten through a neighbor's front gate, how its mother slid between us, ears back, unblinking. I find the library: a room of ancient broken Bibles, their covers torn, their pages bleached illegible. Too decrepit to use but too holy to throw away, the pages have crumbled to a powder that swirls in eddies on the floor. In addition to the Bibles, I find a mop, paper towels, and a few half-empty spray bottles. I consider washing my dishes with paper towels.

I find myself in the courtyard, spongeless. The cloister's official entrance is all wood and iron and medieval bravado, but there's a smaller, more practical door next to it. I slip out the small door and into the road. Halfway down the drive, I turn back to the monastery. The forest swallows it like a snake swallows an egg—peacefully.

Near the road, a sanguine iron statue of some saint rests at the base of the hillside. From the statue, two paths diverge. I take the left one, but almost immediately I hit an overflowing creek and turn back. Pearly water runs down the mountain and under the monastery. The rush of it creates an unsettling sort of white noise, a car forever approaching from behind. It would drown out my footsteps, though, if I had to run away. I could scramble to the tree line, burrow in a hollowed trunk, wield a branch in self-defense.

In my cell, I stuff newspaper rosettes into the back of the woodstove and cover them with twigs. My matches keep snapping against the strike pad so the burning heads ping back onto me. I'm struck by that syrupy animal smell that clung to John in the car: smoke, sweetened by apple bark and newspaper ink. I reek of it. I light match after match, tuck them into the newspaper until the twigs curl in on themselves and the logs catch.

I sniff my carafe, my water glass, my fork. The stench of old sponge makes my heart race.

Whatever quiet power allows me to lie in bed all day and absorb nourishment from the little blue light in my screen like a hydroponic plant should allow me to peacefully endure the passage of time anywhere. The bedroom, the tower, the sanatorium, the holy mountain: It's all the same. I curl up in bed and direct awareness to my hands. Do they feel numb? Am I feeling faint? I can't even google if it's carbon monoxide or dioxide that's poisoning me.

The praying part is easy. It's comforting, to have a place to put my compulsions. I drop to my knees in the Ave Maria room. In the prayer portal in my room, I recite one of two psalms I'd written in a yellow legal pad because my friend Kelly—who grew up more Catholic than I did and is now a professional psychic medium, a one-two punch of spiritual authority—told me they'd help prevent demonic possession. In the chapel I dip my fingers into the bowl of holy water and wonder how long it's been here, if they ever change it out. (Can't google *what makes holy water holy.*) I ask God to protect my Instagram, and animals everywhere, and the membership list of the Italian American heritage social club. I take my medicine: Wellbutrin, pantoprazole, vitamin D, vitamin B12, L-methylfolate, black cumin seed oil, inositol, selenium, lion's mane, magnesium glycinate.

I once watched a reality show in which women were sequestered while they underwent drastic plastic surgery. Separated from their jobs and families, the women weren't allowed mirrors; whoever they were and whoever they would become was at the discretion of the production. In the end the transformed women competed in a beauty pageant. On a different show, contestants were scattered across a remote wilderness with ten items each of preapproved survival gear. It was filmed almost entirely with personal recorders and trail cameras, and the contestants' goal was to survive in solitude the longest for half a million dollars. Some of the contestants openly lamented the strangeness of performing survival on camera, cutting saplings and eating squirrels, piercing the impassive harmony of the wild just to show we can. Monastic sequestration feels a bit like I'm on a reality show and the only viewer is God.

    I watch my coffee crystals dissolve into hot water. I smooth butter onto *biscottes* with the neck of my coffee spoon and then wrap the spoon in a scrap of newspaper so it doesn't touch anything. I experiment with holding a packet of *biscottes* out the window while I open it to keep crumbs off my desk, and the experiment ends when half a slice falls into the private garden. I watch a chemtrail blaze across the sky. I slowly—as wisps of atmosphere twist into a streak of white—identify the smell of melting plastic. On my knees I crawl to the woodstove, the electrical sockets, the kettle. The kettle smells melted. I can't google whether this is an electrical fire risk or a European thing. I write *water heater* in my to-do list under *sponge*. But what would I even do if I found a sponge? Replace it, and pretend it wasn't me? What if there's a policy? What if it hurts John's feelings? When I collected lunch the whiteboard was marked with a trio of ichthyses, and I'm pretty sure that's only because I copied someone that first night, and now someone else has copied me. I unplug the kettle and open the window and lie in bed. If I hold my alarm clock close to my face, watching the second hand skim across its surface is almost as good as scrolling.

A theology of isolation is by necessity outside the bounds of formal education. It's bodily, empirical, ineffable. The penetration of flesh, by sword or spirit, pervades mystical art: Julian of Norwich's visceral, vulvic visions of Christ's wounds; Teresa of Ávila's seraph with his throbbing lance; Angela of Foligno pressing her face to Christ's ribs to tongue his wound. I don't know what to make of this tension between disappearance and embodiment, that the vehicle of sin—the body—might also be a site of divine experience. For Carthusians, the Virgin Mary—a woman marked by her surreal encounter with the divine—holds a particular place of adulation. Notwithstanding the whole virgin thing, one worships her with lush, corporeal language: the seed, the fruit.

It takes three days to find the big garden. It runs parallel to the road, cake-like terraces cut into the hillside behind a wall with a padlocked gate. In a fit of mindful wandering post-lauds, I pass the kitchen and descend a flight of stairs and wedge open a wooden door and then a metal door, and suddenly I'm on a pockmarked stone staircase.

The stairs are slippery with lichen. I scale them sideways to an overgrown terrace, send skittering two lizards who appeared to be—in my uneducated, googleless estimation—fucking ecstatically on a hot stone wall.

The grass in the garden is a dense, suffocating green shot through with new growth. The air is warm and smells like horses.

Everything is awake: whorling buds and strobing butterflies and tiny black spiders that shiver across the ground as I walk. Across the meadow, a waterfall rushes around a statue of the Virgin, the iron pink with age, over a drop grown glossy with algae and into a round reflecting pool. What I thought was a petal floats upward—a powdery moth.

Catholic mysticism is apophatic: It approaches God by negation. There is an acceptance of—a reverence for—the limits of language; the divine is defined by what cannot be said. The thirteenth-century zealot Marguerite Porete wrote in *The Mirror of Simple Annihilated Souls*, "So one must crush oneself, hacking and hewing away at oneself to widen the place in which Love will want to be."

I wonder, in the garden, if what the apophatic theologians were gesturing to was boredom. Boredom: an experience defined by lack. A negative space in the human condition, emptier in some ways than oblivion because at least oblivion is cool. A nothingness that sparks creation. On the contrary: idle hands, devil's workshop. Maybe a practice of extreme deprivation—an experience of radical tedium—is about confronting boredom, enduring it. The path to the waterfall is veiled with daisies and I walk it slowly.

The others and I haunt the cloisters together, passing like ghosts. When I encounter them, I've perfected an expression of deferent indifference: mouth tilted into a soft smile, eyes cast down and to the side. The only real threat of interaction is in the kitchen. The microwave is garishly loud and terminally slow, and when one person is using it there's nothing to do but engross yourself in a teabag wrapper.

No one else looks like they're addicted to their phones, and so they must be very religious or very troubled to be here. The cane-wielding man is cell A, the silver-haired woman is D, and my favorite, the 2009 music journalist, is B. One night, on a moody promenade through the courtyard, I see B photographing plants with a chunky DSLR, and even though it's dark out he doesn't use flash. He looks up and sees me watching him. Something defiant crosses his face before he turns away. A is grandfatherly and affectionate, by which I mean, if I am walking behind him, he will not close the door on me. D is the only one who doesn't mark her meals with an ichthys. I think she's judging my Los Angeles Apparel shirts. Sometimes I pray for them. I'm sure they pray for me, too.

Lunch one day is half a grapefruit and ragout Provençale: carrots, zucchini, eggplant, tomato, and finely chopped bacon, which I spend fifteen minutes mindfully picking out. A decade ago, I read somewhere that pigs can feel hope, and after that I couldn't eat pork anymore. I know that removing the bacon is performative—it's a stew, it's saturated. And anyway, you could argue that the animal is already dead. Eating it is no worse than letting the body go to waste. But isn't that what life is—finding a principle and sticking to it, even when it's petty and pointless in the grand scheme? We're propelled through this senseless and chaotic world by a delicate combination of ethics and willful ignorance in service to the big picture. Leftovers are scraped into a pot in the kitchen and fed to the chickens, John told me when I arrived, and I contribute my soggy bacon even though I haven't seen any chickens.

I scrub my bathroom with an eco-cleaner from the library that I later realize is actually Windex. I wrap a ribbon of toilet paper around the base of the shower head to keep it at an angle, so it doesn't flood the bathroom. I fill my sink with water and squirt in Woolite I'd packed in a travel shampoo bottle. I rub my socks and underwear furiously underwater until the water turns murky. There's a peg for jackets next to the bed and a length of clothesline strung between the legs of the bathroom vanity; I use the clothesline for underwear and the peg for socks, because the peg is in the eyeline of the crucifix. My eyelids pulse with chemical cleaner and the nervous rash I thought solitude could fix. I find a new electric kettle in a closet in the Ave Maria room, but the burning plastic smell lingers. The inside of my mouth tastes like sponge.

At night anchoresses claw their way out of the graveyard and crabwalk up the stairs. Someone hacks my phone and posts a string of slurs. Am I considering that possibility because I want it to happen? Am I bigoted? Is that question indicative of smug liberal ignorance? More than discipline, the thing that keeps me from looking at my phone is a sort of counterdread: There will be so many notifications. In the quiet cell I imagine the numbers on my inbox icon going up and then I imagine throwing my phone into the waterfall.

IN REAL LIFE

* * *

Noise moves strangely in silence. It's magnified and displaced, so you can't quite orient yourself in relation to it. I keep making sounds into other sounds: The wind might be machinery, or I hear footsteps and then it's just the clock. I catch snippets of phantom conversation. I swear I hear someone else's alarm when the window is open, and sometimes when the window is closed, too. Creaks, drafts, the water heater, the stove: everything has a language. The click of the little brass box that holds my rosary. The deafening clamor of keys in my pocket. Footsteps; slamming doors; the thin, otherworldly buzz of the light fixtures. I add *hearing test* and *hearing synesthesia* to my list of things to look up later, which also includes *how thick is soundproof, eye wrinkle normal for 30s,* and *blepharoplasty horror stories.*

What I think is the sound of wings in the wood room is B shaving logs with a hatchet. His face is a mask of serene concentration. The wood splinters but doesn't break. I want to laugh at B, and beneath that I want to protect him, and beneath that, I want to feel anything the way he feels.

D is gone. In vespers, a stranger with a crew cut and pants that zip off at the knee walks straight to her seat. He doesn't know to bow to the crucifix, so throughout the *office* I move slowly for him. I decide he's German and in love with me. *Donnez vos corps aux langues de feu,* we chant. Give your body to tongues of fire.

That night I build a fire in only six tries. I add heat until it turns green and growls at me, and then I shut the door. People make fire out to be this big masculine thing—structure, science, danger—but to sustain a fire, you have to nurture it like it's an infant. Enough balled-up newspaper, and anyone can spark a flame. There's a softness to knowing when to open and close the metal inlet, when to feed and when to withhold. You don't want it to burn too hot, or you'll waste time and wood keeping up; too cool, and it'll blaze out. I'm starting to recognize burn patterns, the way flames sidewind from paper to brush, how different woods smolder, the gentle calibration of tinder and air. My knuckles are black with soot and my pants are white with ash.

The night before the priest comes, I arrive in the kitchen to wash up and find a basket on the serving table. A sheet of printer paper next to the basket reads, *Brioche pour votre petit déjeuner.* Brioche for your breakfast. A test. Am I supposed to take the brioche with me now, as I would *biscottes,* or am I supposed to come back for it in the morning? It might look anxious or greedy to steal a loaf back to the room. But if the brioche was meant to be collected in the morning, why leave it out now? Maybe whoever puts out our food knows that some people don't go down to breakfast in the morning, preferring to stay in-cell; maybe they're just letting us know, so that we're aware we should come down to the kitchen in the morning. Complicating things, they haven't left out any bread plates. I don't know what a normal person would do in this scenario, much less what John and Fabienne expect me to do. No one else's cubby is on the shelf, which means I'm the first one to wash my dishes, which means I must lead the group by example.

Life is endless little choices and their consequences. I'm still washing up when the new guy—C, per the whiteboard—walks into the kitchen, clocks the brioche, and immediately walks out again. He must also be experiencing a crisis of choice. I decide to clean my plate and then, instead of starting a clean plate pile for collection and reintegration into the kitchen, I'll put a brioche on it and take it to my room. I move quickly, and am almost out the door when I brush past C again. Was he watching me through the window? His eyes lock on my brioche. By the time I get to my cell I know I've condemned myself to a night of insomniatic meditation on selfishness.

In the morning the brioche is hard as a rock, inedible.

The priest comes sometime in the afternoon, at which point I may request *le pardon de Dieu*. It's unclear where or how. I write my first note, to John, asking him to ask the priest to visit me. John writes a note back to explain that I should leave a note for the priest, who apparently has his own cubby, with my cell letter. John's handwriting is loopy and sweet and he signs the note with a doodle of a Carthusian cross.

Lunch is a pork chop. It wallows in soft onions and broken cream. It's almost chicken, but it's not. Are the lives of hogs in France more cherished than those in America? If this hog had an upbringing that was peaceful and free, would its consumption be more ethical than that of, say, chicken nuggets? Anyway, who decides what feels hope—if the only way we measure intelligence is against our own, the results will always be skewed. The cream sauce congeals in geothermic rings. I stab the cutlet with my fork and saw off a small piece and hold it to my mouth. The pale muscle reminds me of woodgrain. I feel ill. If I eat it I'll feel bad while eating it, and then after, too, carrying around with me not only the pork but the conviction that I broke one of my few moral codes. It would be a sacrifice, then. Doesn't that make it more noble?

A thin acid of self-loathing creeps up my esophagus as I cut the pork chop into little pieces and push it around the cream sauce. Sour with guilt, I slide the plate into my cubby. I don't want to leave my cell and miss the priest, so I'm trapped with it, the sweaty hunk of innocent pig shut tight in the wooden box like a circus animal.

I'm not sure how far into my cell the priest will come. I shove the cubby under my desk and fold and refold my clothes. Plans to wash and air-dry my period underwear are postponed. In a panic, I shave my legs.

The cell is outfitted with what I'd presumed to be a purely decorative, historically accurate doorbell: a length of wire that runs from the outside corridor into the landing, with the corridor end bent into a noose-like handle. Inside the cell, the wire attaches to a jumble of Chartreuse bottle stoppers and scrap-metal crosses. When it rings for the first time, the sudden thrash of steel and stone is like an ice cube to the asshole.

The priest is short and slight and already peppering me with banter as I open the door. I unfold the slip of paper I prepared in case I got nervous. I recite my intentions: I don't speak much

French, but I'd like to receive God's pardon. When I envisioned receiving God's pardon, I thought maybe the priest would touch my forehead and deliver a brief incantation and I'd be on my way. Instead, he beckons me, impatiently, to walk with him.

He talks all the way down the corridor, pausing for responses I can't give. My already conversational-at-best French devolves into a sort of stream-of-consciousness mélange of high school vocabulary words, homophonic approximations, and English words in a French accent. I feel stupid, slow, and potentially even evil. He asks if I receive pardons often and I say yes, every year, and then I realize I've lied to the priest, and I'm in Mrs. Mortar's classroom again. This thought eclipses whatever the priest says next as he leads me into a small room above the welcome center.

The room is modern and cozy, with a velvety sofa and chairs that don't even look handmade. He sits across from me and knots his fingers and smiles expectantly at me. I experience the distinct swirl of guilt and fear that only comes from a visit to the principal's office. He says my name, or he says *Hélène*, which he thinks is my name, which is fine with me. What is it I want pardoned? I shrug and bite back a nervous little laugh. I didn't think I'd be leaving my cell, so I didn't bring a jacket, and I'm agonizingly aware that my nipples must be visible through my stupid soft bra and stupid slutty baby shirt.

I don't know how to explain the situation with the pork to him, or the situation with the brioche. I don't know how to tell him that it's not even that I want forgiveness for doing the wrong thing, but that I don't even know if I'm doing the wrong thing. Or

I want blazing horny visions, divine contact, and that makes me feel ashamed because I know I'm not special. No emergency exit. What if I did turn inward—what if I found the center, and there's nothing there?

I bet he eats pork. I bet he doesn't even see the problem.

"*Et?*" He's acting like I'm taking up his precious pardoning time with my idiot inability to ask for forgiveness. He seems to enjoy holding God's mercy just out of my reach. He starts rattling off words—ego, violence, hatred, war.

"War!" I say. It's true that I am deeply upset about war, as a practice and a concept. But the priest only shakes his head.

He says something that sounds suspiciously like, "But you can't control that. It's too far away." Is he allowed to deny a pardon?

I don't know how to explain complicity in French. Or the conviction I have that just because I don't have control over something doesn't mean I'm not responsible for it. I feel tricked. Why bring up war at all? You can't uphold the abstract without reckoning with the real. Or maybe you can, and that's what the priest is doing, and that's what I'm doing here too. And even if I can't control war, isn't that the point—that we ask God to take on what we can't handle ourselves?

In exasperation, the priest tells me to ask John to help me write a list of pardons and to come back tomorrow. Not just one; a whole list.

Outside the welcome center, rain falls in italics. I scrape cold pig into the leftovers pot. God's forgiveness feels further and further away from me.

In my cell I update my list—lyrics to the songs that get stuck in my head, translations of psalms, laser vein removal—and sink into a rumination in which my cats run away and no one can contact me. Dinner is mashed potatoes. I eat sitting on the floor, watching the fire.

It's a special mass tonight, with new prayer pamphlets and an incense that makes my rash flare. The priest swans to the altar in tiers of white and promptly goes off-book, either ignoring the pamphlet completely or reinterpreting its order in such a way that none of us can keep up. He has to tell us twice to kneel. It's comforting to realize that he speaks like he's bored all the time; it wasn't just me. We line up for communion and instead of just cupping his hands for the priest, B drops to his knees and presents his tongue.

After communion the priest sings—not a chant, a real song. The thing is: He's amazing. He's got vibrato; he's got range. A holy apparition, two words flash in my brain: *demon twink*. Is the priest camp? I ponder this as the Eucharist dissolves in my mouth, malty and not unpleasant.

In the caustic light of morning, John steeples his fingers.

"I thought it would be a quick blessing," I say apologetically. It occurs to me that John is realizing, for the first time, that I've had no idea what's happening all week.

"You need a…" John searches for the word. *"Péché?"*

"A sin?"

He brightens. "A sin!"

The prospect of identifying my flaws brightens him. He squares the scrap of notepaper I brought him and poises his pen over it.

There are many things wrong with me. I look at John and think about him tagging all the prayer booklets so it's easier to locate the psalms, so we don't feel lost and foolish. I tell him that after I leave the monastery, I'd like to be more present.

"You want God in your life every day." John writes this down, then takes the pen to his mouth. "You still want something he can pardon."

I think back to the priest listing off moral defects. "Ego?"

"*Égoisme*." He writes, thinks, writes and finishes with a flourish. "May God be in my life every day. I ask for God's pardon for ego, and to forgive me as I don't love enough."

John and I find the priest on the stairs to his study. He beams when he reads what John wrote for me.

"*Bon, bon,*" he says. He and John exchange an unintelligible rapport, and we head to the church instead of his office. In the chapel the air is foggy with incense. The priest is buzzing. He dons his whole outfit again. John seems bemused; I get the sense that the priest doesn't put his pardoning robes on for just anyone.

The priest shoos John out of the chapel and leads me to the altar, where he sits on a small throne with lions' heads for arm rests and pulls over a normal chair for me. He reads my pardon back to me. After each sentence I nod and say *oui*, and he nods and says *bon*. He talks at me, and I nod dumbly. He talks about the annunciation a lot—when Gabriel tells Mary she's pregnant—and I'm pretty sure he says this is my annunciation. I nod although I find this deeply stressful. Then he holds his hands over me. He forgives me for not loving enough. He forgives me, he says, for everything.

All empires fall. C is absent from *offices* and I catch John guiding two lanky teenage boys around the microwave. I wonder if they're brothers or friends, try to imagine entering monastic isolation with my friends. When the boys mess up in church I feel embarrassed for them, and then I feel annoyed, and then I feel guilty about feeling annoyed. Maybe they're together because one is very shy, or has a disease, and this is his last chance to heal. The teenagers, with their thin silver chains and normal-width jeans, are a shock, an artifact of the outside world; everyone else here feels so self-contained, like they don't exist outside of this. And as I know them, they don't. I live in a hypothetical here, my life on hold, my relationships suspended. Everything I know about my fellow monks is assumption and projection; we part and the story evaporates. We're strangers.

Shaggy pink peonies bloom in the private garden. I count my vitamins. My eight-day-old napkin disgusts me. I think I have been doing the sign of the cross wrong the whole time.

There is something beautiful in the human urge to build societies, no matter what container we're in. I'm last to get dinner. On the white board the check marks are:

A: ⊂✗
B: ⊂✗
C:
D: +
E: ⊂✗
F: ✗⊃

I sweep the ash from my room. I select my train clothes and roll the rest into little bundles and wedge them into my suitcase. I seal my crumb napkin in a Ziploc bag. I walk around the room, checking for signs of myself.

My last supper is stewed nightshades, a wedge of camembert, and a waffle. I will never know why these meals are so lovingly and confoundingly crafted. Painterly clouds have settled over the valley, lacy at the edges and in the center blindingly bright and dense and white and brilliant. The sky darkens slowly, like someone is wrapping gauze around it. Or around my eyes. With dusk, something washes over me: I'm not going to remember this like it is. There'll be some remnant—but it'll be smaller, darker, like a disposable camera photo. Or there won't be any remembering at all. The quicksand of consciousness will swallow this moment, the clouds sliding over one another, squiggling my vision with their vividness. The valley flickers at the edges. My vision narrows to a pinpoint of rapid motion, to the size of my screen.

When you see a tree moving, you know it's being moved by the wind—but if you'd never seen a tree move before, it might be reasonable to assume it was dancing, or waving, or whatever.

Acting of its own accord. You'd think it had agency. God, biology, anxiety, the internet—maybe I'm animated by some great external force, and I don't even know it. Maybe what keeps me up at night is the illusion of movement when there is only being moved.

I'm changing. On my thumb, a crescent of bare nail visible above the polish. In the kitchen, after dinner, lying in wait for me: a new sponge, clean and bouncy. It almost makes me sad.

I choose a seat on the train that faces my destination. It's not yet noon in France; the rest of my world is asleep. I'll be back on the map soon. This is the last place I don't exist.

I turn on my phone. The solar eclipse in Aries is about to set things ablaze. Celebrate national stress awareness month. Linen is back. It shakes and shakes. It returns to me: indigestion, the throb of carpal tunnel. Some quiet sadness—not because I won't be able to stand it, but because I will.

I search and search. I find the date of the feast of Saint Bruno and the exact location of the monastery and the year of its founding. I find the ten best steak frites in all of Paris. I find the names of birds and flowers in dead languages. This is how I know them. The wind is running its fingers through the trees. The sky blooms and withers, light and shadow. I am not paying attention. I find a translation of the words that marked my cell: *Ecce elongavi fugiens: et mansi in solitudine.* Behold, I fled away and remained in the wilderness.

AN ENDLESS SOUNDLESS LOOP

A BOOKKEEPING WIDOW accompanies her fiancé's brother, a bitter one-handed baker, to a performance of *La Bohème*. They fall in love. A lonely transit worker tricks an amnesic passenger into believing he's her fiancé. She falls in love with his brother. A cadre of teenage boys conspire to turn an artsy girl into a more fuckable artsy girl through gambling and deception. The girl finally accepts the death of her mother, then falls in love.

Sometimes James called me and we synched tapping the space bar so we could watch together. Given the circumstances, it would be easy to say we chose romcoms because they were mindless and heartwarming, but as the global tone shifted from panic into a softer, more sustainable foreboding, I started to think they were neither. The career woman returning to her backwater hometown, the man holding aloft a boombox—how was that different from the witch or the axe-wielding maniac? Romcoms, like slashers, are flashbulbs that irradiate our fears and desires, allegories that allow us to elliptically approach the ugliest sides of ourselves. Bridget Jones crawled up Mr. Darcy's trellis to spy on him through his skylight, and I thought of a girl I'd met in a bar bathroom who ascended two stories of her ex's UCLA dormitory building before she fell to the sidewalk and broke an ankle and six bones in her foot. In the bar bathroom she let us feel the screws beneath her skin. In my bedroom, I repositioned my laptop, laughed when I was supposed to laugh, and considered that somewhere between my spleen and my soul that same unsafe impulse lay dormant, just waiting to wake.

James was adamant he wasn't a cuck. A cuck derives sexual pleasure from the humiliation of someone else fucking their partner; James was into hotwifing, which meant he derived sexual pleasure from the *power* of someone else fucking his partner. Privately, if I had to choose, I believed the cuck was more noble. They got off on the elastic nature of human experience, the way shame and jealousy might twist into a helix of pleasure. It was compelling, the cuck's ability to find that feeling in a situation that wasn't even about them. Not that it really mattered; I was getting fucked either way.

I don't know how long it had been since the borders closed. I knew that for the first year, I was good. We were too scared not to be. I wiped down my groceries and tightened the straps of my mask for my anxious circuitous neighborhood promenades, even when no one was around. When the crematorium was overwhelmed and the air was dense with human ash, I stayed inside. Day to night was a slow shift from gray-orange to black-brown, but my apartment had few windows, so I didn't see it.

My parents have been married for forty years and still love each other. I asked my mom how she knew my dad was the one and she said to me, "Anyone else I'd ever dated, if you held a gun to my head and said, 'Marry him,' I'd have said, 'Pull the trigger.' Your dad was the first one where I wouldn't have rather been shot in the head."

horny for being adored 🌷 would love a nice dinner 🐌 in an open relationship. I chose emojis that were rococo but not overly childish. I chose softcore photographs: a satin sheath of plausible deniability clinging to my tits, a smile that could be joking.

 I dispensed identical flurries of nudes, not caring if they were clearly from different time periods, if the color of my nail polish didn't match or my laundry pile moved around. Men loved to ask about my Canadian boyfriend, and I loved to tell them about our tragic separation. My devotion made me both boring and utterly enticing, like a packet of silica gel.

 At some point, like Victorian sweethearts, everyone got into constitutionals. Walks were not only safe, but an efficient way to get to know someone: If my date complained that certain types of people kept junk on their lawn, for example, perhaps they were insensitive to the generational trauma of diaspora, and not only was that generally shitty but it meant they would probably be insensitive to whatever generational trauma had been planted inside me that year, the latent seed of horror waiting to wind its roots through my children and theirs and theirs. James wanted detailed descriptions of every encounter, screenshots and photographs. He didn't like the walks because there was no potential for sex or sexting.

James was adamant that the borders separated us, and so that's what I told men on the internet. In reality, I'd sent him the email address of an immigration attorney when he first landed in Los Angeles, six months before the borders closed. I followed up and he told me not to pressure him and it went on like that until James's papers expired, two weeks before I bought my first hand sanitizer. And so, the borders kept us apart, yes, but it was also the visa, and it was also whatever was in James that prevented him from sending the email. "We could just get married," he'd said, the day before his flight.

What gave me pleasure? Very little, but enough. My friends, my kitten, roses, spaghetti, great art, White Claws, online shopping, bad TV, the moon. I wasn't pessimistic or closed off; the way I saw it, I was *too* open to the world. I was desensitized to it, like how in health class they teach you chronic masturbation desensitizes you to sex. I had rubbed too vigorously up against art and music and poppies unfurling on highway medians at dawn. What could romance offer me after that?

When I said I wanted *a nice dinner*, I meant the simulation of a dinner date. I meant a contract of suspended disbelief: For a few hours the world hadn't ended, and we were two normal people having an unexceptionally nice time. They arrived with damp paper bags of curries and dumplings. We fumbled over small talk. I unfolded my paper napkin and smoothed it over my lap. Sometimes we would just eat and talk, happy for conversation. Everyone I met was refreshingly unselfconscious about their desperation. It was the feeling of heavy turbulence, when your stomach drops and, without thinking, you reach for the hand of the stranger sitting next to you.

The hotwife is an object; the kink is pride of ownership. Sometimes James was frantic, badgering me to set up a date with someone, and sometimes he was petulant and jealous. Sometimes I lied to him, fabricating trysts when really I'd just watched hours of *SVU* with my notifications silenced.

Even before James's proclivities intruded, I was a person of the internet. I knew that I didn't fully own myself. I loved the thrill of meeting new people, the power of unavailability. After a while, though, even nice dinners lost their sheen. I bantered about depression and the inattentive government and the end of the world with the same titillated despondency I felt when I scrolled Britney Spears's Instagram: it was no longer fun to be in on the joke. I moved my body and tried to imagine how I would describe it to James later. I thought of that art piece that was just a shark submerged in formaldehyde. The artist who made it was known to be an asshole.

* * *

Time was moving strangely. The message was new, but when I opened it I saw it'd been sent three days ago. What am I making for dinner?

I felt something akin to how tigers at the zoo must feel when a new rubber ball appears in the enclosure. No one had ever offered to cook for me.

I flicked over to the messenger's profile. MG's face was angular but boyish, dusted in seven o'clock shadow. A mischievous face. He lazed on a fawn leather sofa, a bored gray cat in his lap, wearing the sort of hypebeast fuckboy T-shirt that I didn't associate with men who knew how to cook. He laughed in a suit at someone's wedding, looking sweetly adult. He stood at the foot of a staircase, his arm around a somber brunette. Into jazz, bread and ENM.

Ethical non-monogamy: the more enlightened nomenclature for open relationship. He'd probably read *The Ethical Slut* and had a suite of rotating secondary partners drawn up like a chore chart. Ethical non-monogamists could be techy or neolib or cringe, but I'd found that many of them understood the basic tenets of consent, and that relationships could be both casual and respectful. Plus, there was a calming delineation to being someone's other. It was romance with a run time, a repository for desire without risk.

Years ago, before everything, I'd been a waitress in Brooklyn. One night at last call I was rolling silverware at the bar next to two drunk guys deep in a conversation about love. They slid off their stools and groped around for their jackets and one drunk guy slurred to the other, "No man is an island," and the other guy said, "Yeah, but two people can be."

I lived on the back side of a strip mall across from a Pentecostal church, behind a defunct hair salon that was wedged between a bodega and an insurance agency. The entrance to my apartment was a narrow corridor between said salon and insurance agency, hidden from the street by a corrugated metal door. There was no bell or buzzer; guests had to text when they were outside and I'd come get them, and usually they were lost halfway up the block. My landlord owned the insurance agency. A romantic, he'd adorned the side of the building with a looming photorealistic portrait of his wife's face. It was hard to shake her judgment.

Leading up to dinner with MG, I swabbed my mouth at the baseball stadium and waited for negative results. I sent my two best friends his phone number and a brief description, so they could file a report if I disappeared.

I cleaned the litter box and opened the kitchen window, even though it faced the brick wall of the bodega. I looped and unlooped the top button of a silk blouse I'd bought a decade ago at a thrift shop. I couldn't tell what level of undoneness better conveyed insouciance. The lead-up to meeting a stranger is always a rush. Whether or not the date goes well, you'll never be strangers again. The lighting (a sad arrangement of floor lamps), the Spotify playlist (SZA), the blade of eyeliner (sharp): Everything vibrates with potential. This is the last moment you control everything. And then your phone buzzes, and your life is different.

AN ENDLESS SOUNDLESS LOOP

The Pentecostal church had started meeting in the parking lot. They played saxophone late into the night, jazzed up by the end times. I crossed my little porch and cut past the yard to the unlit corridor, backed by the horns of rapture. Everything smelled like wet asphalt. The gate was a dense mesh, designed so you couldn't slip prayer pamphlets through its links. On the other side, bathed in streetlight, MG came into clarity gradually. Very tall. Holding a large box.

The big box and small passageway meant we couldn't hug. I led him, Orpheus-like, into my kitchen–slash–living room–slash–office. MG pulled a frosted plastic bag of rocks from the box. Oysters. He'd apprenticed at a bakery in Germany, now worked in artisanal sourdough, and had a seafood friend who'd done him a favor. He'd brought tomato soup and the fixings for grilled cheese sandwiches and some obscure Bavarian cookie, too. I'd planned a few icebreaker anecdotes, but I felt giddy, suddenly, puttering around my kitchen with a cocktail shaker that sloshed cold gin all over my hands.

I stood over the sink and MG handed me an oyster swaddled in a dish towel. He wrapped my fingers around the wooden shaft of a stout double-edged shucking knife. "Like this," he gently rocked my wrist. The top of my head slid under his chin like a tongue into a latch. I envisioned blood, emergency rooms, the story he'd tell his girlfriend about the strip mall urchin who hemorrhaged into his martini. "You got it," he said to me. "Nice job." Its insides were nacreous and quivering.

★ ★ ★

I knew how to compartmentalize. Like many a yearning-racked teen, my pleasure was shaped by Tumblr: a violet storm cloud rolling across the plains of the girl internet, the first propagator of the erotic gif. If the purpose of porn was to show sex, the purpose of the gif was to reframe it. Frequently uploaded in black and white and thus vaguely vintage and romantic and French, the erotic gif was an endless soundless loop divorced from context and meaning. There were money shots, sure, but most compelling was the before or after: the perpetual falling of a bra strap; the radically oversized cock, spitted to the shine of rock candy, easing its way along a milky thigh without ever reaching its destination. To be in love, or at least in pleasure—to feel anything so deeply that you unclasp yourself from time in devotion to space—I'd hone my life to a pinprick of light, a tiny box of infinite movement, if it meant I could feel that way forever.

that was so fun! glad you're home safe I texted MG at 3:09 a.m. He kissed like a needle kisses a record player: a soft sigh of contact and then blood-rushing, riotous noise. In the quiet of my apartment, I flossed. I dotted my jawline with moisturizer. I was unattached to outcome.

When I woke, MG had texted me a YouTube video about European gardens. I responded with a playlist of songs composed for plants, so he sent me the Wikipedia article for John Cage's composition *ORGAN²/ASLSP (As Slow as Possible)*, which was apparently twenty years into a 639-year-long performance in a church in Germany. Memes, internet gossip, sexting. Layers of blue and gray spiraled upward the way mineral drippings accumulate into stalagmites in a cave. Our cave: away from the contaminated and closed-down city, on the sidelines of our relationships, inside the remote rectangular confines of my apartment and the remote rectangular confines of my phone.

What did I love? The yard. The yard was an expanse of yellowing grass overlooking the bodega parking lot. I shared it with my upstairs neighbor, Carla, who was the only other person on our whole block because we weren't technically residential zoned. Once we'd started a petition to lift the street parking restrictions, and even though we got 100 percent of the resident signatures, the measure didn't pass because officially, we didn't exist.

Carla and I planted sunflowers along the chain-link fence and got roaringly drunk on chillable reds and took turns ordering drugs from our preposterously hot drug dealer and his waifish delivery girls. We smoked or snorted whatever and tried to untangle whether he was sleeping with one or all of them, and whether he would ever sleep with us. I took in a stray kitten from the bodega alley, and we fed the bigger, more feral cats wet food spooned into empty takeout containers from my dinner dates. Occasionally we dragged plastic kiddie pools out to the middle of the lawn and lounged like Venusian beauties.

I was Kirsten Dunst eating a salad and MG was Jake Gyllenhaal watching me. I was a Gemini corgi and MG was a Sagittarian horse. We were two rats surfing a telephone wire, two coyotes shining their watermelon eyes across a dark boulevard. The most romantic word in the English language: *us*. We could be anything. There was no future anywhere, and so we had nothing but the playful, sprawling present. We talked about our morning routines and humiliations and little hopes, compared star charts and search histories. I called him from Grocery Outlet to read aloud the names of off-brand products. He arrived straight from work with delicate lemon tarts and loaves of bread that smelled like clean skin. In my bedroom the two of us were one electric jellyfish, a pulsing loop of light suspended in a soft dark sea.

MG texted me a photo of his cat—the gray one from his profile—looking haughty on that leather sofa. It would be easy to miss, if you focused on the cat: the soft slope of a knee, clad in heathered sweatpants, breaching the left corner of the frame.

I never asked about MG's girlfriend but never shut down conversation about her, either. In turn, I tried to neither obscure nor showcase my relationship with James. What little information I had was a haphazard mosaic pieced together from these radically relationship-neutral exchanges: she had a name that was often shortened, but even people who knew her well used the long version. She'd suggested opening the relationship. They lived in South Pasadena. I wasn't allowed in their apartment, but I knew from the background of a FaceTime call that she had a shelf of cream and beige books lined up in one long gradient, like in the homes of *clean girl* aesthetic influencers. They'd been together for ten years. "It must be special, to know someone for that long," I'd said over oysters, and MG said, "I guess so," and I recognized something unnamable in the way he said it and changed the subject. MG was a realist; he had accepted that no one could offer everything to anyone. He, too, could compartmentalize.

I zoomed in on the knee. Maybe they were talking about him texting me, in the convivial, generous way that ethical sluts talk about their lesser conquests. Maybe she got off on it. Fine with me. I had the MMA fighter who showed me his collection of occult texts and goddess figurines; the copywriter bro from the west side who traversed four different freeways to argue about leftist politics; the skater-slash-DJ for whom my tepid interest was a drug, and who oscillated between ghosting and confessing his love for me. Sushi, tacos, steak au poivre. When the test schedules didn't sync up, they sent delivery, dick pics. An endless loop of flirtation and chatter and dishes soaking in gray morning light. They were like shoebox dioramas of relationships, small and complete and controllable.

"Did you cum for him?" James would ask on the phone, his voice sparkling with static. In LA, James had been amazed by the number of hand-painted storefronts, the colorful lettering on bodegas and party supply stores and burger shacks. The thing about James was, he was the last person I loved before the world went dark. On the phone, I searched for the feeling of driving through the city, pointing out hardware store signs. Most of those stores were closed.

I whispered, "I came for you."

* * *

I spent hours copy-pasting emojis into elaborate scenes that I called *emojiscapes*: swaying grass and shooting stars and clouds and waves and mushrooms and turtles and swirling planets. MG responded with comets and dynamite and red telephones. Life on a tiny red planet.

"Is this him?" James once asked about a writer I'd seen a few times. Armed with the man's first name, a vague job description, and an untold number of hours, he'd found his Instagram. "He's so weird looking. He looks like a fucking loser."

I told James not to make fun of my dates, and he told me I was choosing them over him, I didn't even miss him. Maybe this was part of the game too. He loved asking me who I had sex with, but more than that, he loved hating them.

This was a diversion, though, because I was the unethical slut. I wanted something for myself—some current of desire that didn't immediately flow to someone else. I wanted to hold a charge. I didn't tell James about MG.

MG and I pushed hot dogs onto coat hangers. I'd heard the earth was healing itself; I pictured gossamer threads of ozone weaving themselves into a fine lace far above us. On the earth plane the Pentecostals had invested in a megaphone, so wails of rapture wove themselves into the wails of sirens. Behind MG the sun swelled red. I willed it to burst.

"You look like a snow bunny," MG hooked a finger into the sleeve of the fuzzy sweater I'd bought just so he'd touch it. "I wanna take you on a ski trip someday."

A plan. A crack in the container. Our date was loosely cowboy-themed, and so I'd beseeched the owner of my local liquor store for the speckled ceramic promotional mugs that came boxed with an expensive bottle of whiskey. I'd secretly pre-boiled the hot dogs so we didn't get food poisoning. I had attempted and abandoned homemade graham crackers. I was invested in the fantasy of the present. And then casually, luxuriously, MG spoke of the future.

"I don't ski," I said.

"I'd stay in the chalet with you," he said. "Have you tried real fondue?"

We watched a horror movie. I walked him out in the early morning. He sent me a podcast about pilgrimages, and I sent him an Anne Carson essay on walking the Compostela with a man who doesn't love her back. What were we to each other? We were two strangers sending more smoke into the ash-filled atmosphere, roasting hot dogs over the coals.

I FaceTimed James, and his room was dark. A lamp had broken. "Can you get a new lamp?" I asked.

"It's not that easy," he said. "You always think things are so easy."

I turned my lamp off too and we sat in the dark. We were pixels and photons. We were four thousand miles apart.

"It feels like we're not in a relationship anymore," he said.

"I know," I said.

It died quietly.

* * *

On the night of the hunger moon, we left the apartment. The only thing MG told me was to wear sneakers. His Prius was well maintained and a little messy, like him. I fought a feral impulse to leave something behind—a tampon, a hair tie.

MG took us north, from the big highway to the little one to the winding boulevards of La Cañada, where no one drove even in the daytime. We talked about cybersecurity, how we do and don't want to become our parents, how we feel bad we no longer talk to our childhood friends. When we talked it felt like we were reaching so deep inside ourselves that we'd meet somewhere on the other side, like dropping a quarter in a manhole so it falls out the bottom of the earth. The connection was irrational, quantum. MG wound us up the mountains and the car dissolved into darkness, just the soft beating of two voices batting nothings back and forth.

There are people who look up and see stars every night, but I wasn't one of them. I loved the wavy heat lamp sunsets of the city; I felt like a lizard in God's terrarium. On the one lane set slack against the trees of Angeles National Forest, the moon's brightness was eerie and penetrating. We were stupid, I thought, to think we had any right to name the moon.

MG turned into a crescent of dirt at the edge of some mountain. He parked and got out, and I got out too. Below us were curtains of forest and then a basin of light.

He procured a portable speaker and a black orb. He fiddled with the speaker and the canyon was drenched in LCD Soundsystem. He pushed a button and the orb began to spin, shooting red and green and blue lights into the trees.

"Dance party at the end of the world," he said.

Museums and concerts and natural wonders elicited a vicious loneliness in me. In the presence of real beauty, I always felt like I was looking at the right thing, standing next to the wrong person. The stillness, the searching, the awareness that something is unfolding in front of you: you have to feel that alone.

MG noodled his long arms, a graceful fool, and I didn't feel lonely. There we were: an island. He drove us back in the middle of the night, past the sleeping bobcats and the blue-lit 7-Elevens, his hand on my thigh, the black road rolling under us like a tape unwinding.

If obsession is an attachment that's unique or unusual, then you kind of have to be obsessed with someone to have any sort of crush—he's *just some guy*, and you're thinking about where his hands are in space. You're wondering if across the city his hands are in a shape that might conform to the shape of your body as you lie in bed rotting and dreaming. (Of course, this doesn't apply to parasocial or celebrity crushes, who aren't just some guy; you could argue that their socially agreed-upon romantic value makes them less eligible for obsession. They're impersonal placeholders, which is why they are such good romcom protagonists.)

In a damp nest of sheets, in the quiet minutes before MG had to leave, I was gripped with feelings I'd only associated with non-romance things: the wonder of tiny bubbles floating upward from the Dawn bottle, the thrill of making eye contact with a stranger's dog. In his absence I scrolled through our texts with the intensity of a TV cop scrubbing surveillance footage. I was looking for clues—confirmation that this was what I thought it was. Under the harsh lens of my lust, MG's words receded into glyphs and shifted around. He was never confusing, which was more confusing. After a torrent of sexting he wrote, **Fuck I just want to hold you so tight.** When his car got rear-ended and I offered him mine for the day, he returned it with new windshield wipers. He wrapped his hand lightly around my throat and murmured, "I've never felt like this before."

That was the problem: It was so easy. It was like sliding into water the exact temperature of your body. It was like when a familiar song comes on the radio and you don't realize you're singing along until you hear your own voice. And then he left, and things became deliriously difficult. Sometimes I felt like a lab rat jackhammering a buzzer for more validation, withering away, my fur falling out from lack of sustenance. Starving even as I gorged. The evil delusions of romcom heroines lurked in my mind: *This could work.* And logically, I knew it couldn't.

I imagined telling my friends that I thought my hookup might leave his girlfriend. I imagined their faces: chevrons of worry at the corners of their eyes, teeth bared in a taut balance of enthusiasm and apprehension. *Not for me,* I always emphasized. I was a *girls' girl.* I never looked his girlfriend up on Instagram or returned to her picture on his dating profile. It felt violating, somehow, even though she probably chose that photo. I wasn't in denial—if anything, I felt that to know her was to legitimize our comparison, to insert myself into her life when I knew my place was in the periphery.

AN ENDLESS SOUNDLESS LOOP

From our brief conversations, I gathered that they were something akin to platonic life partners. It was my understanding that MG had initially been resistant to opening the relationship; soon after he agreed, his girlfriend started dating her coworker, who was also someone MG knew and had to see around sometimes. MG never complained or shit-talked her; I tried not to Frankenstein his benign comments into a monster to justify my lust.

I made pros and cons lists. I bought and burned love candles. I watched reruns of *The Bachelor* and I wept when the women craved words of affirmation. On *The Bachelor* they were always saying they wanted to *do life with someone*. I realized that, like the personal trainers in their pageant gowns, I wanted to do life with someone too.

In romantic comedies, the credits roll because the stolen lover is a rotten prize. Nothing ill-gotten can last. Maybe the central horror of the romcom is how deceit and violence and subterfuge are inextricable from true love, which means that to be in love, you need to be a little awful.

I hovered my face an inch from MG's and telepathically communicated: *My heart is full of pop rocks. I feel a deranged bliss when I trace a heart on your nose with my nose. I want to be bored with you. Watching you suck the air from a Ziploc bag before putting it in the freezer makes me think you'd be a good father.* I said, "You're fun."

When the white tents came to desolate high school parking lots—when the vaccine came—MG texted me, I'm so happy, we're gonna tear this town apart this summer.

Some greater power took to my stomach with a handheld drill. Soon, it would be apparent how we didn't fit into each other's lives. His Wi-Fi router was named for someone else's inside joke, the password someone else's pet. There would be restaurants that implicitly belonged to his primary partner, weddings at which I would not be the plus one, parents who would never know I existed.

In my most degenerate intrusive fantasy, I ran into MG and his partner at karaoke. I had no choice but to take the stage, and the song that had been chosen for me was Robyn's "Call Your Girlfriend." I surprised even myself with the richness of my voice, my sudden ability to hit the high notes. I made eye contact first with MG, and then with his partner, and in that moment we reached an understanding. After the applause died down we complimented each other's hair, discussed the latest *New Yorker*. We all laughed about this, the delusions and insecurities of the monogamous, while palming tomatoes at the farmers market. We made a summer salad and ate it in a field à la Ina Garten. Did she and Jeffrey swing?

I was as unwell as Bridget Jones climbing Mr. Darcy's trellis, but I was not Bridget Jones. I was the menacing young lawyer who appeared to steal Mr. Darcy away. No matter that after Bridget is briefly detained in a Thai prison for reasons only tangentially related to the film's romantic engine, the young lawyer reveals that she's been pining not for Darcy, but for Bridget all along—when we audition, we don't always know the role. The end credits flashed before me. MG had given me exactly what I'd wanted. I had to ruin everything by wanting more.

I needed to confess in the most ethically slutty way I knew how, which is to say, on ecstasy. MG had said he'd wanted to try it; I rationalized that I would be able to speak from the heart, but really, I wanted the feathery cushion of psychedelia to pillow his rejection. I wanted one last night in the eternal present. To squander tomorrow's serotonin tonight—wasn't that what we'd been doing all along?

I curated a playlist and arranged my softest blankets on the bed. I bought knockoff Pedialyte from Grocery Outlet and a six-pack of Corona from the bodega. I made space on my bedside table for the little orb from our dance party at the end of the world. And then my phone buzzed, and my life was different.

We sat cross-legged on my bed and waited for the come-up. We were giggly, conspiratorial. My fingers slid through his, catching at the tips.

I asked, "Would you be seen in public with me, in the new world?"

MG paused. "I already told my friends you're my girlfriend. I hope that's okay."

"But you have…"

"A partner."

A rush of wind. No—the sound of me sucking up air. The sound of dust sinking into my comforter. My dry mouth. If I breathed out I would start to cry. I tried to focus my rapidly expanding pupils on his. I'd meant to wait until I was receptive and reasonable. I'd meant to cushion my fall.

"I can't," I said. "I mean—you made me realize I want these things, and now the problem is, I want them." And there it was: Our lives clicking to the next frame. "I can't be your girlfriend if I'm not the only one."

MG looked out into the room, into the future. Acid rose in my throat. He turned back to me.

"I know," he said. "I need to..." Slowly—so slowly—he nodded. "I think we need to see this through." His hand on the back of my neck, in my hair. "It's so obvious." His eyes like broken glass bobbing in the ocean, before it's battered into something smooth. "You're it."

And then we disintegrated.

In name and chemical structure, the synthetic psychoactive phenethylamines MDMA and MDA are nearly identical. Their only variance is a single hydrogen atom in place of a methyl group, a stray hyphen at the end of the sterile honeycomb arrangements that are abundant in internet image searches. MDMA and MDA both elicit feelings of euphoria, belonging, heightened stimulation, and heightened tactile sensitivity. Both were on the menu that our dealer sent over Signal, and so maybe Carla had submitted our order with a typo, or maybe someone had put an orange smiley face sticker where a yellow smiley face sticker should be, or maybe the lovely delivery girl was new and her grasp of the smiley system was not yet refined—whatever transpired, it was understandable. We wouldn't know something had happened until the next morning, when I could consult Carla and Google and confirm that we hadn't, in fact, consumed MDMA. We'd consumed MDMA's more potent, longer-lasting, more amphetaminic, more hallucinatory cousin, and if you didn't know the difference, it would be plausible to assume, in the moment, that you were actively dying.

All those silly photos we'd texted each other were true. We were two live wires snapping on hot pavement. We were two dragonflies skimming a still pond. We were a million particles that had cycled and recycled through history, and every breath was an exchange of the crumbs of eternity. Every breath was a lifetime. We had the ash of the dead in our lungs. We were going to need an ambulance.

"Is this normal?" MG asked.

"Uh-huh," I said.

I put my clammy hand over his staccato heart. *What are we?* What a crazy question. We were two colored lights chasing each other like bunnies through the meadow of the future.

"It's the eye of the needle," I said.

"Hhhnnn," he said.

The disco lights rolled over my headboard and through my mind flashed a photo we'd taken that night in Angeles National Forest. We were sweaty and beaming, and the flash only reached as far as our faces. Beyond us, the flat black of some great chasm. We were over the edge, suspended in time.

"Stay here," MG said.

"I'm here." I put my ear to his heart and there we were: two people dying. Two people who couldn't save each other, but could at least bear the broken together.

YOU HAVE A NEW MEMORY

* * *

On the other side of the come-up was bliss. Our eyes started to adjust and our hearts found their rhythm and my faux sheepskin rug felt thrilling. We walked into the yard and watched the streetlights fizz gold onto the pavement. We touched our bare feet to the yellowing grass and told each other we meant everything.

On the other side of bliss was the comedown. We drank Gatorade and watched a documentary about mycelium. And later MG texted, **Made it home, gf.**

I thought, *I am not dying. I am living. This is what it feels like to live.*

IT ENDS
AND IT ENDS
AND IT ENDS

(ON GLORY)

I COULDN'T EVEN grieve on time. I scraped my tires against the curb, fed the meter before remembering it was Sunday. The rules kept changing on me. The rug shop was one of a row of quiet storefronts on a street that was busy in the Los Angeles way: many cars, no pedestrians. Its sign was flipped to *Closed* but the door was unlocked. Through the front window you could see a herd of brass camels grazing on a white display stand and a pile of shoes by the door.

I wore novelty socks from CVS with pixelated ponies whose faces twisted garishly over the knobs of my ankles, embarrassing because they were both excessively ugly and excessively synthetic.

In the back room, rugs had been arranged in layers across the floor and rolled into corners and flung over wooden rungs that climbed up the walls to the ceiling, padding the space like a womb or an insane asylum cell: bright geometric weaves and muted knits so plush and snowy that I half expected them to bleat when I brushed them with the back of my hand.

On the rugs sat twenty or so activists, artists, journalists, students, baristas, urban planners, and project managers, plus one woman who had just returned from living off-grid in a post-capitalist community in Costa Rica. I was offered a floor pillow and a cup of lemon balm tea poured from a silver pot into a tiny red glass etched with gold. It always makes me anxious, those first ten minutes sitting cross-legged with strangers. I didn't want to mingle. I wanted our intimacy blunt and contained, like casual sex. It's more honest to me that way.

I have this idea I keep returning to that I call *plastic bag theory*. Basically, the internet, like a plastic bag, is a container that is both disposable and forever, and when we use the internet we become disposable and forever too. We've long associated permanence with greatness: the bronze statue, the gilded death mask, the naming of streets and rivers and lecture halls. Plastic bag theory concerns a new permanence. A permanence of shame: mutilation, mutation, the enduring stain of violence on both that which is harmed and those who harm it. I am both a flimsy vessel and an agent of destruction. It's not even a theory, really; it's just a smart-sounding way of labeling how the future used to feel like a sheet of blank paper and now the future feels like an envelope, like its corners have been creased and folded in on themselves. The envelope contains something, but I can't say what.

I can't pinpoint the moment we agreed the world was ending. The height of the pandemic would be an easy guess, but then I recall carbon emissions and oil spills and the jutting ribs of a polar bear on a gently spiraling ice floe. I recall the almost-rapture of 2012, when a Bible Belt misapprehension of the Mesoamerican Long Count calendar catalyzed prophecies of solar maximums and boiling planets and inky supermassive black holes that would devour our constellations in front of us as we gazed at the night sky. I recall the dawn of the millennium, barely: the vibration of adult anxiety, a pitch I could barely register. I was a kid and fell asleep before midnight. I recall other nights, watching the leery reverend Jim Bakker dip a ladle into the Creamy Potato Soup Bulk Bucket ($160 plus shipping) or the 30-Day Fiesta Bucket ($100 plus shipping), Tammy Faye next to him, purring about Christian genocide, her hair a curl of butter on a bone china plate. But it never ended. Every time, the tragedy happened to someone else. The comet veered its course; the Instagram story flicked to an ad for ketamine therapy. Every time, a soft exhale—relief, tinged with disappointment.

At some point, though, doom became room temperature. Doom is the muse for environmental reportage and giddily nihilistic memes and hand-wringing opinion pieces; doomscrolling is an entire sector of online activity. At first this felt radical: Despair was the last online space that couldn't be made corporate. It wouldn't be strategic, from a marketing standpoint, for Coke to express guilt over the permanence of its cans or draining potable water from Chiapas. And anyway, to speak an experience is to diffuse it. I saw an infographic that delineated a new glossary of eco-dread: *eutierra*, feelings of euphoric interconnectedness; *solastalgia*, mourning or sorrow for a specific place; *eco-phobia*, avoidance or inaction caused by eco-anxiety; *eco-rage*, anger caused by eco-anxiety; *tierratrauma*, trauma of land or earth. It can't consume you if you consume it first. I scroll the way a dog rolls around on a dead animal.

Doom and its handmaidens are so pervasive that researchers have begun assessing hopelessness's practical application in the world; they wonder whether we can harness despair, like wind or water, and convert it into energy. "It has been found that climate emotions do indeed influence behavior significantly, but the dynamics seem to be very complex and there are no simple solutions to these practical questions," writes ecological grief researcher Panu Pihkala. "For example, various researchers have argued whether guilt or pride would be a better motivation for pro-environmental behavior, but recent research suggests that this may be case-dependent."

The climate grief group was a space to luxuriate in emotion. It emphasized validation. It was free of calls to action, lectures, or advice. It was an anti–fight club, closed to conflict and open to all, although none of the participants around the teapot was older than forty-five. Our leader was twenty-four, with slim hands and a soft, earthy voice that reminded me of charcoal. "Every other space is focused on action," he told us. "This is about *how* you're doing, rather than *what* you're doing."

Our leader procured a small bowl of plant cuttings and asked us to go around the circle and choose a plant with which we resonated. One by one, we shared with the group what drew us to the natural object, and what drew us to the rug shop. It was a conservative talk show's wet dream: a circle of coastal hippies playing show-and-tell and worshipping seedpods. I pictured a bead of sweat rolling from a teased combover down a pale neck into the red garrote of a necktie. Our delicate, laughable distress. It was my turn. The group was patient; it seemed like they actually wanted to know why I had come, which panicked me. The bowl contained leaves of various interesting shapes, a sliver of palm frond, a wedge of soft bark.

I came because incorporating doom into the mundane had not brought me comfort. It was irresponsible to avoid anguish, to allow the right meme or recycling strategy to pacify me. I couldn't look away. It kept me up at night, as it should, the way I drifted around destroying things until I inevitably settled into one garbage patch or another.

I selected a small clipping of purslane and, at a loss, explained that it seemed like it would have a good mouthfeel.

The problem with the end of the world, besides the world ending at all, if it's even ending, is that the facts are overwhelming, abstract, upsetting, boring. I don't want to list them out, because who does that help? You already know. These are the things I know: Whatever year you read this will be the hottest year on record. A heat wave is bad, but a heat dome is worse. I ingest, on average, five grams of plastic a week, which is the equivalent of a credit card. The rapid thaw of permafrost reawakens viruses and bacteria, so if you don't drown, you'll probably be poisoned by anthrax. Since 1970, wildlife populations have declined by 69 percent. California, where I live, lost 39 percent of its forests between 2000 and 2020, and an additional 13.5 percent between 2020 and 2021. Sometimes in fire season the sky is the orange of safety vests, which feels ironic. It was a mistake to treat the planet as something disposable and forever; apparently, it is neither. The apocalypse will not contain closure.

Philosopher Timothy Morton understands climate collapse as a *hyperobject*, a term they coined to describe "massive nonhuman, nonsentient entities [that] make decisive contact with humans, ending various human concepts such as 'world,' 'horizon,' Nature, and even 'environment.'" Hyperobjects exist at the edges of human perception and perspective; they are both under our purview and out of our control. They are epistemologically sticky—leaving their trace on everything—but they are also nonlocal: they are so large and so massively distributed across space and time that humans can only engage with them indirectly. In addition to global warming, Morton's examples of hyperobjects include black holes, evolution, and the sum total of all Styrofoam on Earth.

I would add to that list: the internet. I am unable to conceive of the physical servers that run software and databases, and so I refer to it as one omniscient entity, *the cloud*, pervasive but impalpable.

Approximately four hundred million terabytes of data are generated every day, an ever-increasing deluge that induces a sort of permanent brain freeze. In response to the speed and quantity of information, we've developed a survivalist comprehension model: for faster metabolization, facts are streamlined and compressed, opinions whittled to their sharpest points. When I think of the cloud, I think of an incomprehensible amount of space that stretches outward, unfillable, no matter how much we add to it—space, but no time. No time to grapple honestly with complex concepts like God or all the Styrofoam, nor the sprawling seismic waves of oceanic temperatures, nor the pulsing circles where the bombs dropped nor the exasperated text post that reads WHY ARE WE PRETENDING THIS IS OKAY.

I understand the urgency, the blame. In the rug shop, I basked in the glow of righteous vitriol. We lamented the poor choices of boomers, the apathy of parents, the ineptitude of therapists. Around and around. Annoyance rippled through me. One woman expressed resentment toward a friend who had thoughtlessly absconded to Bali, and I felt angry at the friend but also angry at the speaker for lounging in a rug shop instead of mailing a pipe bomb to the CEO of Shein.

I ping between resenting others and resenting myself, anguish over a plastic straw before remembering that one hundred companies are reportedly responsible for 71 percent of global carbon emissions, and then sinking into nihilism because it doesn't matter if you recycle or not, but the thing is, you still need to recycle. The best way I can describe this cycle is *leash aggression*, a common behavioral pattern in which otherwise socially adjusted dogs become aggravated and hostile when leashed. It's a problem of compounding conflation: The leashed dog sees another dog and lunges toward it; the collar tightens against its throat; the dog associates the other with the sensation of choking; it lunges harder. The dog: able-bodied straw enthusiasts, members of the grief group who indulge in meandering tangents, my future self who would drive away from the grief group in her energy-inefficient vehicle. The collar: oil barons, politicians, tech billionaires. It's ill-advised to bite the master. It's a waste to be angry at someone who doesn't care if you have hatred in your heart, because they don't care about you at all.

One definition of glory: a clock that measures ten thousand years. The Clock of the Long Now is the stuff of blockbuster sci-fi, a leviathan timepiece built into the side of a mountain and owned by Jeff Bezos. The Clock of the Long Now was initially imagined by computer scientist Danny Hillis; the first prototype is currently under construction on Bezos's private land in Texas's Sierra Diablo mountain range. The clock will be synchronized to solar noon and stand five hundred feet tall. If all goes to plan, it will tick once a year, and every millennium, reveal a cuckoo.

Stewart Brand, a founding board member of the Long Now Foundation, says of the project,

> Such a clock, if sufficiently impressive and well-engineered, would embody deep time for people...Ideally, it would do

for thinking about time what the photographs of Earth from space have done for thinking about the environment. Such icons reframe the way people think.

The goal of the Clock of the Long Now, then, is to reframe the consequences of our actions as generational, rather than immediate; to help us metabolize the vast scope of human existence, so we better survive.

Jeff Bezos's legacy corporation, Amazon, reports a 34 percent increase in carbon emissions since 2019. In 2021, the company produced 709 million pounds of plastic waste—a chain of plastic air pillows that could circle the Earth over eight hundred times.

Who is time for? The clock's construction necessitates decimating a section of the Sierra Diablos, a mountain range whose oldest rocks formed in the Precambrian age roughly one billion years ago. Blasting them apart to build a testament to ten thousand years seems profoundly human.

I stumbled upon the grief group on Instagram—a post with the meeting schedule, set to R.E.M.'s "It's the End of the World as We Know It (And I Feel Fine)"—while researching ways the average person might survive the apocalypse. Most of my research time was spent perusing the online catalog of Atlas Survival Shelters, the "Worlds #1 Bunker Builder," which fabricates a range of shelters from the BombNado to the Platinum Series luxury line. You can buy a sandblasted steel box with a bulletproof hatch or a concrete dome shelter starting at $20,000. A gun vault door is an additional cost, as is a toilet. There is proprietary carbon dioxide scrubbing technology and a nuclear, biological, and chemical warfare package. There is a bunker one enters through one's kitchen island that, until the barbarians are at the gates, doubles as a wine cellar.

My closest brush with self-reliant living was when I visited an old high school friend who lived and worked on an organic strawberry farm up the coast. She wore a bandanna pulled up over her nose like a bandit because she was allergic to everything. She showed me the strawberries and the chickens and the pigs and her gun and the vast rows of strawberries across the road, which she said was a Dole farm. Because her farm was organic and Dole was not, a hardy breeze could blow pesticide-laced dirt onto their land and compromise their certification, and Dole didn't seem to care, so much of her work was tarping down her strawberries whenever the wind picked up. She showed me an old drum washer with the lid ripped off and told me that after slaughtering a chicken, putting it through a spin cycle was the fastest way to pluck it.

I read about the fantastical escape plans of the upper class, the resources poured into developing biohacked hardiness and robot militiae to better escape the suffering masses. For left-leaning or cash-strapped preppers, you could take a climate futurist's "personal ruggedization" course, starting at $149—only fifty dollars more than a Jim Bakker Black Bean Burger Bucket—with instructions for assessing the apocalyptic viability of various American regions, surviving on a budget, and protecting one's family.

I briefly considered traveling to a Preparing the People rapture prepper conference in the Mormon haven of Rexburg, Idaho. I pictured myself intrepidly infiltrating the conference, exposing America's hyperindividualist paranoia while holding space for bright flashes of empathy. I didn't go to Rexburg because I'm neither charismatic nor Aryan-passing enough to be anything but an interloper, and because the conference was canceled after one of its repeat keynote speakers, a fringe Mormon fiction author named Chad Daybell, along with his wife Lori Vallow, murdered Vallow's seven- and sixteen-year-old children in an apparent doomsday cult ritual.

I lined up interviews with climate scientists and journalists and policy experts. This was the great sadness, maybe: that even if I could parse the data and disseminate the infographic, I would not be equipped to act on that information. And yet something must be done; the end of the world is an existential crisis without the luxury of philosophical distance. *What would you say to a layperson?* I asked them, and what I meant was *What would you say to me?* I didn't know how to explain that I felt like a plastic bag, not in the Katy Perry way but in the nihilistic despair way. I wasn't sure how to ask what I actually wanted to know, which was *How can I be sure there's a point?*

The industry of preparation, like the internet, runs on an engine of urgency. It is always already too late. The future, then, is a foregone conclusion, decreed by God or your least favorite president: a conveyor belt that ends in flames. I, too, am not immune to timing, to the frail and needy human body, its fears and its reckless frothy hope. Maybe I never made it to Rexburg because I was afraid I could be pacified. Maybe I crave absolution, too.

In the rug shop, I thought about what it would be like to be rolled up in a rug, like a corpse pre–body dump. Safe, probably. Peaceful. A man was talking. "I'm here because I want to remember to be empathetic," he said. "People say action is the antidote to anxiety, but action's also an impediment to empathy." My turn again.

I wanted to say I have done so much work to want to live. I have taken honest inventory of the broken circuitry of my mind, soldered frayed connections in the ruby haze of cortex, dry-swallowed the pills, sat in encircled plastic chairs, assessed my intrusive thoughts and interest in daily activities on a scale of one to five. I have filled in the correct circles with ink, which in turn always fills me with a downy sadness, same as on the dentist's inpatient questionnaire when they ask you if you like your own smile. I wanted to live—and now the twist: It was the planet who would give up first.

I said, "I want to have a baby."

On TV, the baby-crazed woman is overwhelmed with love for children, any children. They come to her in dreams, dance for her, reach for her with angelic chubby arms. She wants to cradle them in her arms. She wants to rip them from the stomachs of strangers, rinse the blood off, and raise them as her own. For me, it was body horror. The hum of planned obsolescence, the clock running out—a stale and slightly offensive horror that I knew was the limp-dicked figment of a 1970s pseudoscientist's imagination, but I felt it anyway. My own personal doomsday clock. All around me, suddenly, were babies. I didn't want to hold them. Instead, I was struck by the paranoiac suspicion that people were having babies *at* me.

I never experienced a *desire* to procreate—just a heavy animal ache that reminded me I was a vessel, a breeding bitch, one of those porcine dogs at the dog park with heavy swollen teats, the kind you are embarrassed for even more than the dog that runs around licking other dogs' assholes. My baby craziness was a degrading, depersonalizing, warm animal impulse in the way that a crush is a warm animal impulse. It was pleasurable in the way that a crush is pleasurable—the pleasure of being flattened by your own base needs. I was in heat. And this meant that at my biological core, I was not a nihilist at all.

It's bad magic, though, to cast a spell on an unwitting subject, even a money or love charm. That's a bit how the creation of new life felt: good intentions applied to a nonconsenting party. Not a curse, exactly, but a sideways blessing. I checked out a book from the library that purported to help with the decision of parenthood. Its epigraph included quotes from Ralph Waldo Emerson and, forebodingly, Nietzsche. The book posed queries like *Do you crave the attention lavished upon pregnant women and young mothers?...If so, consider other ways you could enjoy receiving attention more easily*, and delineated a guided meditation in which you imagine you're carrying a backpack that contains your life's ambitions, and then you imagine a baby in the backpack, and the baby throws your dreams on the ground. *Are you happy about this? Would you, perhaps, consider fumbling the baby?* Another exercise suggested that Mary Shelley wrote *Frankenstein* as an allegory for motherhood and invited the reader to envision birthing a literal monster.

One section, "Metamorphosis," split questions between those who would experience pregnancy and their partners. For the pregnant: *How do you think your partner would react to your changed body? Do you worry about whether he'd still be attracted to you?* The following section was titled "Suckling" and continued this line of questioning for husbands: *Imagine your partner nursing your baby. You're sitting beside them. How do you feel? Proud, turned on, jealous?*

These questions were ostensibly for people who could blithely affirm that they did not fear the future. The book didn't even cover the credit card's worth of plastic.

"We manufacture all sorts of survival shelters used to protect you and your family," reads the Atlas Survival Shelters website. Many prepper resources put children at the forefront of their messaging. If you're going to have a child, you should be prepared to encase them in concrete, to protect them from the world you created. Atlas Survival Shelters' home page boasts a photo of three towheaded children and their beaming mother piled on a black suedette sofa. The mother ducks to better fit in the photograph, and to avoid the metal ladder that cuts above her head.

The saddest part about the bomb shelters isn't the invocation of bombs, but how depressing they look—like you'll survive, but then you have to eat Fiesta Buckets in a white rectangle with little or no internet. Maybe it would be worse if there were internet, if you rehydrated your beans and watched the carnage aboveground.

Add a few windows, though, and that's what I do now. Hence the grief group.

I was grateful that the group forbade advice. I just wanted to say it out loud—to grieve the future, whether I got what I wanted or not. Motherhood is a type of Armageddon too, I've heard. It's terrifying, to become the feared unknown—not to traverse it, but to become it. To let the body be overgrown with new life, to sacrifice the old territory for the sake of sustaining its new inhabitants. I have a friend who got pregnant and needed a special prescription toothpaste because her fetus was sucking the calcium from her teeth. And yet there it was: some primal want. Desperation, which must be a form of hope.

When I interviewed climate experts, I didn't ask them about children, but I did ask them about the future. My subjects were not concerned with rapture or artillery stashes. The general consensus was that my limited understanding of the data was correct—we were fucked—but the scientists weren't nihilists. Regarding climate collapse, Tamma Carleton, an environmental and resource economist at UC Berkeley, put it practically: "I wouldn't dedicate all of my time trying to figure out what we can do to solve it if I didn't think it was solvable, because then there would be no point."

It occurred to me that it was not only agonizing to think of the future as a foregone conclusion; it was selfish. And it begged the question: Who defines apocalypse? How many people, and of what value under capitalism, does it take to end a world?

"I think that there is an assumed newness of the apocalypse

on the part of predominantly white interlocutors, or in the way that the apocalypse is positioned in Hollywood and popular culture," Secwépemc and St'at'imc writer and filmmaker Julian Brave NoiseCat told me. "It's often some sort of invaders from space, or some sort of ecological collapse…It's positioned in those narratives as something that has never happened before, but there have been histories of invaders coming to new worlds, destroying the ecology and environmental relationships in those places and those worlds. There are multiple groups who have experienced the apocalypse and near total destruction of their worlds in their own way."

Another kind of glory: After the 1948 ethnic cleansing of Palestine, the Jewish National Fund intentionally planted European conifers over the villages they'd razed. Only 10 percent of Israel's forests date from before 1948, and only 11 percent of the forests' trees are indigenous species. Marketed as an environmental initiative and a boon to Israel's fledgling timber industry, the project's true aim was antirepatriation: verdant obliteration. Forest as forgetting.

There are churches and nihilists and bomb shelter websites that will tell you the future is a resource, like money or land, and there is not enough for everyone. I think there is no future—only the present, stretching like taffy in all directions. The unplasticking of oneself, perhaps, is a radical acceptance of mortality. It's a process in service to that which will outlive you. My interview subjects did not speak of futuristic tech or distant solutions, separated from us by space and time; they spoke of neighborhoods, communities, improving quality of life here and now. "I think that a really good way of thinking of the work that needs to be done is trying to be a good ancestor now," said Edgar Reyna, a climate resilience analyst in the Los Angeles mayor's office. "Like, okay, my grandparents left me this. I'm their descendant; they're my ancestors. Whose ancestor am I going to be? It's a powerful approach to considering reparations and considering climate action and policy now, and then individual action for the future…We want urgent action now so we can have long-term success."

On glory, Ilan Pappe writes in *The Ethnic Cleansing of Palestine*:

> At times, the original flora manages to return in surprising ways. Pine trees were planted not only over bulldozed houses, but also over fields and olive groves…But this particular species failed to adapt to the local soil and, despite repeated treatment, disease kept afflicting the trees. Later visits by relatives of some of Mujaydial's original villagers revealed that some of the pine trees had literally split in two and how, in the middle of their broken trunks, olive trees had popped up in defiance of the alien flora planted over them fifty-six years ago.

My brother is an atmospheric chemist. He spouts depressing statistics like "humans spend more time indoors than some species of whale spend underwater" and analyzes the chemical composition of farts. Looking for whatever I was looking for, I texted him, **i am hoping for something approaching reason and honesty, even if** it's opaque or boring. i guess i want someone whose job it is to parse the future to tell me how people who aren't tech billionaires or alt-right preppers should prepare for it.

He texted back, That is easy. you should actively tend to your close relationships, be open to new friendships, treat others as you would wish to be treated, and often perform acts of kindness and sacrifice for complete strangers. But science won't help with this.

There is nothing I learned that can heal you. I was wrong to ask for a point—or I'd misspoken. What I had meant by *a point* was an ending, some solution. A point on the horizon. You get to a point. There were no answers; there is no ending. This doesn't mean there's no point.

Maybe someday I will be resilient. Maybe this will mean I feel less, or maybe this will mean I am heartbroken over and over again and I keep feeling it and survive. Maybe the big earthquake will come before fire season, maybe after. Maybe I'll have a kid. Maybe they'll read this. In that future, I want to say: I cannot prepare you. I do not know what time will mean to you, but I'll give you mine. I will tell you about what we couldn't save. Life will slip through your fingers—you must make it again and again and again. I know I won't be able to save you. I will try to let you feel pain. I will try to find meaning in that. I believe there will be things worth saving. I'm sorry. I love you. I hope you like it here.

AUTHOR'S NOTE

As Henri Laborit put it, "We could almost say, a living being is a memory which acts." Conversations have been reconstructed to the best of my ability, or drawn from texts, emails, and other first-person documents. Names and certain identifying details have been changed or obfuscated, even for those who don't deserve it.

ACKNOWLEDGMENTS

Thank you to my editor, Maddie Caldwell, for holding my hand and matching my freak. Your brilliant insights, infectious enthusiasm, and ability to delicately convey that no one needs six thousand words about a leaf were invaluable. Thank you to Morgan Spehar, Dana Li, Lori Paximadis, Anjuli Johnson, Carolyn Levin, and everyone at Grand Central for bringing this book into the world with skill and grace. I couldn't ask for a better debut author experience.

Thank you to my agent, Marya Spence. Your sharp eye, almost-scary expertise, and unwavering belief made this book possible. Thank you to Mackenzie Williams and the team at Janklow & Nesbit for your thoughtfulness and encouragement ushering this book into the world.

Thank you to Francesca Billington for your impeccable fact-checking. Thank you to Julian Brave NoiseCat, Tamma Carleton, and Edgar Reyna for taking the time to speak to me and for lending me your expert thoughts on climate collapse and hope (or hopelessness) at the end of the world.

ACKNOWLEDGMENTS

Thank you to the luminous writers and artists who lent their support to this project in its earliest stages: Nada Alic, Lucy Dacus, Shelby Lorman, Sarah Lyn Rogers, Reggie Henke, Hallie Gould, and Ursula Ellis. Thank you to Phoebe Bridgers for championing my early work, untangling the meaning of justice in various hot tubs, and telling me to stop punishing my younger self. Thank you to Nina Raj for always having a staggering number of climate resources on hand, and for always being down to engage in witchcraft in your yard. Thank you to Emma Carpenter for literally rescuing the manuscript and for educating me on club drug chemical compounds. Thank you to Haley Dahl for inviting me to your ghost town Christmas party. Thank you to Rachel Antonoff for believing in my ability to write both horny product descriptions and literary nonfiction. Thank you to Corley Miller and Rachel Ossip for talking me through these essays before they were essays. Thank you to my perfect friends who read typo-ridden drafts, let me vent in the group chat, and offered solace, walks, and natty wine, including but not limited to: Leah Clancy, Keisha Raines, Claire Donovan, Cecily Glouchevitch, and Chrissy Tolley. I love you.

Thank you to my parents, Kathy and David, for your faith, and for loving me even when you don't understand me. Thank you to my sister Phelan for reading my legal documents and to my brother Caleb for texting me about the apocalypse.

Thank you, Matthias, MG, my muse, collaborator, critical eye, and confidant. You balk when I say I couldn't do this without you, but the truth is, I couldn't do any of it without you.

Thank you, reader, for making this memory with me.

ACKNOWLEDGMENTS

Thank you to my editor, Maddie Caldwell, for holding my hand and matching my freak. Your brilliant insights, infectious enthusiasm, and ability to delicately convey that no one needs six thousand words about a leaf were invaluable. Thank you to Morgan Spehar, Dana Li, Lori Paximadis, Anjuli Johnson, Carolyn Levin, and everyone at Grand Central for bringing this book into the world with skill and grace. I couldn't ask for a better debut author experience.

Thank you to my agent, Marya Spence. Your sharp eye, almost-scary expertise, and unwavering belief made this book possible. Thank you to Mackenzie Williams and the team at Janklow & Nesbit for your thoughtfulness and encouragement ushering this book into the world.

Thank you to Francesca Billington for your impeccable fact-checking. Thank you to Julian Brave NoiseCat, Tamma Carleton, and Edgar Reyna for taking the time to speak to me and for lending me your expert thoughts on climate collapse and hope (or hopelessness) at the end of the world.

ACKNOWLEDGMENTS

Thank you to the luminous writers and artists who lent their support to this project in its earliest stages: Nada Alic, Lucy Dacus, Shelby Lorman, Sarah Lyn Rogers, Reggie Henke, Hallie Gould, and Ursula Ellis. Thank you to Phoebe Bridgers for championing my early work, untangling the meaning of justice in various hot tubs, and telling me to stop punishing my younger self. Thank you to Nina Raj for always having a staggering number of climate resources on hand, and for always being down to engage in witchcraft in your yard. Thank you to Emma Carpenter for literally rescuing the manuscript and for educating me on club drug chemical compounds. Thank you to Haley Dahl for inviting me to your ghost town Christmas party. Thank you to Rachel Antonoff for believing in my ability to write both horny product descriptions and literary nonfiction. Thank you to Corley Miller and Rachel Ossip for talking me through these essays before they were essays. Thank you to my perfect friends who read typo-ridden drafts, let me vent in the group chat, and offered solace, walks, and natty wine, including but not limited to: Leah Clancy, Keisha Raines, Claire Donovan, Cecily Glouchevitch, and Chrissy Tolley. I love you.

Thank you to my parents, Kathy and David, for your faith, and for loving me even when you don't understand me. Thank you to my sister Phelan for reading my legal documents and to my brother Caleb for texting me about the apocalypse.

Thank you, Matthias, MG, my muse, collaborator, critical eye, and confidant. You balk when I say I couldn't do this without you, but the truth is, I couldn't do any of it without you.

Thank you, reader, for making this memory with me.

ABOUT THE AUTHOR

AIDEN ARATA is a writer and artist whose writing has appeared in publications including *BOMB*, *Mask*, *NYLON*, *The Rumpus*, *The Fanzine*, *Wonderland*, *Hobart*, and others, as well as *NDA: An Autofiction Anthology* (Archway Editions, 2022). Arata's visual and video work was showcased in Kunsthalle Bremen's bicentennial exhibition, "Generation*. Jugend trotz(t) Krise" (Bremen, Germany, 2023), and has been featured on platforms including *VICE*, *The Cut*, *Harper's Bazaar*, *Mashable*, NBC, *Seventeen*, and *The Washington Post*. *You Have a New Memory* is her first essay collection. She lives in Los Angeles and on the internet as @aidenarata.